ENTERPRISING WOMEN

ENTERPRISING WOMEN

The Lives of Successful Business Women

CAROL DIX

BANTAM PRESS

LONDON · NEW YORK · TORONTO · SYDNEY · AUCKLAND

TRANSWORLD PUBLISHERS LTD
61–63 Uxbridge Road, London W5 5SA

TRANSWORLD PUBLISHERS (AUSTRALIA) PTY LTD
15–23 Helles Avenue, Moorebank, NSW 2170

TRANSWORLD PUBLISHERS (NZ) LTD
Cnr Moselle and Waipareira Aves,
Henderson, Auckland

Published 1991 by Bantam Press
a division of Transworld Publishers Ltd
Copyright © Carol Dix 1991

A catalogue record for this book is available from the British Library
ISBN 0593 022467

Typeset in 11/12½pt Century Old Style
by Chippendale Type Ltd., Otley, West Yorkshire, England.
Printed in Great Britain by Mackays of Chatham, PLC, Chatham, Kent.

ACKNOWLEDGEMENTS

To EMBARK ON a book of this nature could lead a writer into a state of terminal anxiety. It is all very well having the initial idea: the brilliant concept that out there must be so many Enterprising Women, that all is needed is to bring them together to explore the various problems and privileges they have experienced. But where to find these women? Will they want to talk? Will they be prepared to divulge their innermost secrets to the outside world? Or at least to myself?

To that end, I must thank all the women with whom I have had friendly or professional contact, who so kindly and willingly passed on names of suitable subjects or, more than likely, waxed lyrical over someone else's brilliance, endurance and strength. As anyone attempting to research this area will find out there are no neat sources of reference, no statistics, no mailing list of women running their own businesses. Names were given to me through various networks, from differing sources. I would like particularly to thank *Options* magazine which, in partnership with the TSB, has been running the prestigious and much-coveted 'Women Mean Business' Award for several years. *Options'* chief editor Jo Foley and several of the other editors were more than helpful in supplying me with names of previous winners. Similar awards and incentive schemes are run by *Cosmopolitan* and *Good Housekeeping* magazines.

Women's networks are always a good source of ideas and contacts. And I would like here to thank the then-chairman Ann Kelly, secretary Liz Harman, and members of *Women in Management* for unstinting help and support in my various efforts. Another source of leads came through an offshoot of Network. Yet others came from my contacts with professional business graduates previously met in my book, *A Chance For The Top*.

Lastly, I would like to thank Pat White whose early-start business attempts and my involvement in this new-born dream, led to the idea of writing such a book. And, just in case I forget them, a special word of thanks to my own very enterprising young women Alice and Yasmin, who will, one day, emerge into their own truly powerful new-woman's world.

CONTENTS

Preface   ix
Introduction   xi
PART 1: STARTING UP   1
1. THE START-UP: LESSONS FROM
THE FRONT LINE   3
   Dounne Alexander-Moore   7
   Emma Bridgewater   19
   Penny Phipps   29
2. DEVELOPING A FAMILIAR BACKGROUND   39
   Airdre Taylor and Annita Bennett   41
   Nuala Forsey   51
   Anne Rigg   59
3. COMING IN FROM THE COLD   69
   Vivienne Pringle and Judy Lever   73
   Gillian Harwood   83
   Jan Morgan   91
4. THE DOGGEDLY INDEPENDENT STREAK   101
   Fiona Price   105
   Linda Stoker   115
   Judy Farquharson   123

PART 2: WHERE TO GO NEXT 129

5. STAYING SMALL: THE POSITIVE APPROACH 131

    Anne Calleja 135

    Yolande Beckles 143

    Hilary Sears 149

6. RAISING CAPITAL: SELLING ON 155

    Suzy Frith 159

    Victoria Barnsley 169

    Susan Hay 179

    Prue Leith 189

Epilogue 197

Appendix: Company Names and Addresses 201

PREFACE

So, is the 'enterprise culture', the baby of the Eighties, already dead? The question has to be asked as we move on in the Nineties, many of us at the helm of our own fledgling or well-entrenched business.

The business women featured in this book would be unlikely to see themselves merely as part of an off-beat idea dreamed up in daredevil times. I would hazard a guess that they are a symbol, rather, of the great changes that have taken place for women in the past two decades, whereby women grow up to accept that they will have careers as well as any form of domestic life to look forward to.

The fact that so many women seem to be opting for a work life, over which they retain total control, should not disappear behind closed doors. Therein lies much for us to ponder, as we reflect on demographic changes, their effect on the workplace, and the interest shown by both men and women in finding different ways to work.

Before going any further, let me offer a little chronology. Most of the interviews for this book took place in the late summer and autumn of 1990. The recession that seemed to dawn with 1991 had not yet been seriously witnessed. There had been no war in the Gulf; though interest rates were cripplingly high, and major voices were sounding portentous about the problems shortly to be met by businesses, both large and small.

The comments made by the women featured in this book were true for the period in which they were mentioned. Each business was contacted again in the early part of 1991, to check for accuracy and to alter vital factual errors. There was a moment, I will confess, when I feared the worst. Would several of these women already have gone out of business? Would recent gloomy talk have taken a stranglehold? But no. They all sounded, to a woman, cheerful, cautiously optimistic and definitely looking forward to the way clearing in the near future.

Women are resourceful and resilient. Accustomed to being flexible and accommodating changes within personal relationships, they are undaunted by the larger changes and external pressures of the world. If the women whose lives and businesses make up this book are an example of womankind in the nation as a whole, then we should know where to look for our country's vitality and its future!

These women and their businesses were chosen to appear in this book, not for any specific reason, other than their being kind enough to give me time for a very lengthy interview. I was looking for a wide selection of women from different backgrounds, with varying viewpoints and stories. I asked them all to speak naturally, to include as much personality and humanity as possible in their discussions. The dry bones of business theory can be picked up from text books. In *Enterprising Women*, I wanted other women to be able to learn by example, rather than being given rules or set directives. What has emerged could be described, I suppose, as a 'slice of life' book. Personally, I found these slices highly educational. I trust the reader will agree.

INTRODUCTION

THE TERMINOLOGY OF small business, words such as *entrepreneur* and *enterprise*, have become almost clichés in our present-day world. From government exhortations to the unemployed, or those fearing redundancy, to get 'on their bike' and create their own destiny, to the banks' seeming desperation to encourage people to start up on their own, we are indeed living through turbulent times in the working world. Individuals set out on their journey through life, well aware that they are unlikely to stay with a firm, as a trusted employee, who will one day leave with his or her gold watch on retirement.

Starting up your own business, whether as a small-time one-woman operator, or determinedly setting out to create a sizeable business concern with many full-time staff of your own, is a likely and feasible part of any adult life. For women, it seems, the chances of such a personal and highly individualized mode of work or attempts to meet success are even greater.

The figures, such as they are, reveal that one out of every three new business start-ups these days is initiated by a woman. One quarter of all the self-employed are women. Indeed, the exponential growth rate of numbers of women becoming self-employed in the previous decade shot up by 137 per cent. In case we fear our laziness, a higher proportion of women now work in Britain than in any other EC country, except Denmark.

All of this goes to prove a point: many women are now seeking employment, whether married, with children, or single. And if, in the current working world, the number of hours involved, the promotional and job-satisfaction levels available, are not within women's own boundaries, then they will leave and set up on their own. And, more than likely, they will make a success of the venture.

One of the purposes of this book was for me to prove what at first I only imagined to be true. Women's businesses are no longer small-time ventures featured in cosy magazine articles about, for example, a 'perfectly lovely' jam-making business in the Cotswolds, established on the back of the successful husband and basically supported by his greater financial gains; nor are they domestically based at-home trades carried on within the limits of school hours.

The women currently starting up businesses, and those who have been quietly plugging away for the past ten years or so, are a determined bunch: ambitious, serious-minded and surprisingly successful. They may keep the size of their business small, in their own terms, believing in the ethic of 'small is beautiful'. But small to one woman might mean a turnover of a few million, when she is comparing herself to a turnover of one hundred times that size!

Another basic motive behind this book was for me to delve into the question of why running a business seems to be such an attractive option to so many women. Is the answer to be found in that, by being her own boss, she can juggle the hours available in a day between home/family needs and working demands? Or is it because so many women find themselves taking years out of conventional working lives to raise families, only to discover when they contemplate a return, that they no longer fit into a corporate or bureaucratic structure, because they would have to accept far too low a salary and work that is at too lowly a level?

Or is it that too many women still suffer from the 'glass ceiling' effect, feeling stultified in their desire for a greater sense of control over how far and how quickly up the ladder they can move?

Do women, essentially, just not fit into what is still a very male club – the working world?

The answers can be found, from the evidence of my small sample, in all these reasons and more. There are women featured here who did not *know* they had the strength and stamina to set up a thriving business, nor were they armed with the necessary knowledge and experience, until the breakdown of a marriage or some other disaster forced them towards survival stakes. There are other women who decided, while very young that, rather than work for someone else, they just wanted to set up their own concern, to be their own boss.

Indeed, who can say exactly why we make such moves? Women tend not to have been groomed by loving parents, nor by school or mentor, for the role of entrepreneur. Yet, they appear to have a natural empathy and desire for just that style of working.

While researching the book, I spoke to several women who had already moved on beyond the immediacy of the entrepreneurial set-up; women who can now look back and reflect on various issues involved. Lady Judith Wilcox, at present chairman of the National Consumer Council, has been a business woman all her life, having set up, managed, and eventually sold off two major companies in the west country fishing industry. Brought up in Plymouth during the War, she sees nothing overly remarkable in her achievements, merely that her own path, like that of so many women, followed in the footsteps of generations of natural-born entrepreneurs.

'In the fishing industry, because the captains were out at sea, it became quite natural for the women at home to run the family businesses. My great-grandfather died with his ship. He left my great-grandmother with nine children and a fleet of fishing boats. She continued to run the business from the shore. For my part, while my father was away at war, my mother turned from fish to investing in property. So it was really a very natural decision, when the right idea came to myself and my first husband, that we start out in our own business. At that time, we were importing *langoustines* from Brittany to Plymouth.'

As Lady Wilcox implies, running one's own business is an instinct that comes naturally to many women; one with which maybe we have lost touch. Back in the nineteenth century, and even earlier, women ran local businesses: they rented out rooms or operated hostelries; they took in washing, made clothes for other people, took care of children. Women have always tended to rule their own homes, to be comfortable within that power base.

Indeed, even as we congratulate ourselves on the successful running of a business, we should be careful of complacency. The ability to find power, or control, within our own companies will not solve all women's problems. As a nation, we still need more women to contemplate finding their place and power base within the major corporations and public bodies.

The idea of researching *Enterprising Women* grew out of my previous book on women business graduates (those pioneering souls who had studied for an MBA), *A Chance for the Top*. Having been very impressed by these high calibre women, who had confronted such major issues, as pushing their way to the top of the corporate ladder (and who were able to command salaries in figures that I just did not associate with women in the work-force), I was surprised to hear from many of their lips that the one goal they were working towards was 'one day to run their own businesses.'

Putting the idea of such a goal as a test question in the context of that book, I considered whether it meant that:

- women are at heart natural entrepreneurs, gifted with an individualism that drives them away from the rigidly structured work-force to go off on their own.
- women are forced into this desire because they just cannot fit their working hours and domestic lives into the structures imposed by an outside work-regime. Does the notion of working for themselves, or running their own companies, afford them instant flexibility, even if it might lack outside recognition and status?
- by going it alone, women are giving up the fight to make the male work-place adapt to their needs rather than persisting with slow change from within.
- working for yourself is more 'feminine' and working for a corporation a more 'masculine' ideal or tradition.

Hilary Cropper is chief executive of the very successful high-tech company FI Group plc. Originally founded by Steve (Stephanie) Shirley back in the early Sixties, FI was formed to tap into the massive numbers of highly trained female computer programmers who, nearly thirty years ago, found that once they left work to begin a family they were unable to move back. FI was one of the first companies to network home-based women workers. The company has done extraordinarily well over the years: a privately owned plc with shareholders mainly from within the workforce they now have a turnover running at around £18 million.

One of the reasons for its continuing growth and success was Steve Shirley's decision in the late Seventies to delegate much of the responsibility for how the company would evolve, by bringing in a chief executive from the corporate sector. Hilary Cropper had worked her way up the managerial ladder, and then she made the move to FI from ICL.

Does Hilary Cropper believe that a small company such as FI could have grown to such an extent without the imposition of tactics from the corporate world? 'A company has to reach a point where it needs new skills that have been acquired from a different culture,' commented Hilary Cropper. 'One of FI's strengths has been in employing people to perform specific management functions. It is such people who take a company through to the next stage. Richard Branson, for example, has hired very good executives to take Virgin forward – people who are certainly not in the mould of high-profile entrepreneur as himself.

'The entrepreneur or founder tends to enjoy the smallness and intimacy of what they have created. They find themselves upset with the type of procedures that have to be imposed. They may view these as bureaucratic, where in fact I see them as essential. Entrepreneurs may prefer to hang on to the camaraderie, the feeling of being intimately connected to his or her staff. Once you head up a sizeable concern like this, then you are very much on your own. Any chief executive will tell you the same, man or woman. It is by your decisions that the company will stand or fall. However, I have to admit that I find such high-pressured, high-stakes work great fun! Though, you do need nerves of steel.'

The women, whose lives and working practices are studied in this book, are by default entrepreneurs. They have given highly personal and tangible accounts of just what drove them to set up on their own, what problems they may have encountered, how they broached the basic hiccups such as whether to borrow money before starting up or to let the business grow and expand naturally; and what they imagine the future holds for them.

None of the women omitted details of her emotional or domestic life. Even if I did not push the questions that way, each woman volunteered the information. A woman's private life, whether she is married, single, has children, would like children, is divorced; whether she has found herself abandoned by a partner, has pushed out the man she saw as ruining her life, or continues to live in peaceful harmony with one supportive partner, that reality forms a framework for each life. It is not something that women overlook.

Work is never seen by women as a totally separate picture. They integrate their working lives with the rest of their lives. That must explain ultimately why so many want to run their own businesses, because only in that way do they feel more in touch with their whole life.

Whether a woman is more likely to run a business while she is still single, when she has the support of a partner, or, if the motivation comes more often when she is spurred on by having children, these are also highly individualized concerns.

From my own sample cross-section, I can offer the following statistical survey: out of the women originally interviewed, 3 are single as yet without children; 4 are divorced (or single parents) with children in their sole care; 12 are married and have children; 2 are married, so far without children.

As for their ages, they cover a broad spectrum: 10 range from their late twenties to late thirties; 8 are in their forties; and 3 are over fifty. But then it must be remembered that I have deliberately interviewed women at very different points in their lives. Some are just starting out, while others have been in business maybe twenty or more years.

Twice as many of the women had left former careers before starting their own business, while others had either had temporary jobs or had been housewives beforehand. Five out of the sample did not have children; yet only six of the women with children felt their prime reason for going off on their own was because they could not fit full-time work round giving as much time to their young children as they felt was necessary.

The women themselves gave their own reasons for why they wanted to run a business: they used words like control, flexibility; they needed to put more into or get more out of their working lives; or they spoke of seeking a 'quality of life'. Some expressed the feeling that they had achieved a certain degree or level of income as a salaried employee and either felt they could earn more or achieve more on their own. Others just decided this was what they wanted to do and to hell with anyone else's advice!

Tina Knight, founder and managing director of Nighthawk Electronics, a 'small' business rooted in the green heartlands of Essex (indeed it is based within the grounds of her own home), is a well-known figure within the business world, who has recently been appointed vice-president of the Small Business Bureau – the only female voice on the Board and a position she relishes with enthusiasm. Outspoken, funny, charming and attractive, within five years Tina has taken her own business in manufacturing computer peripherals from more or less nothing to a turnover of £2 million. Does she have an opinion, I asked, why her own and so many other women's businesses are surviving, when all around her others go to the wall?

'Maybe because we care less about preserving our own status. I have noticed that failure of businesses very often comes along behind too strong an ego, or greed. I have not over-borrowed. The business has expanded rapidly, but it has been controlled growth. I have a healthy turnover, but to others that may seem small. Yet, I know that my profit margin is high. As they say, "turnover is vanity, profit is sanity." I was talking recently to a man in business who has an annual turnover of £25 million. Sounded great until he told me he makes a loss of £500,000 a year on that!'

Most women seem to concur on the point that as a gender we do not crave power, glory and ego-boosting status symbols as much as men. We can live without titles such as 'vice-chairman' or 'director'. When a business does well in its first two years, a woman is less likely to be seen buying the latest Porsche or sports saloon. She may well stick to her old Renault or Mini, and feel that she would not dare risk so much money on something as foolish as a *car*, until she felt very secure.

Instead, the women's ambitions emerge in a different light. For example, several women interviewed here talked of future dreams which lay beyond the business currently created. They did not dream of running a chain of stores, or owning the biggest manufacturing plant, or earning the greatest millions. Rather, they had plans to write a novel, become a broadcaster, to travel round the world, or even sell out and start up a completely different project. They were greedy, I would say, for new challenges and responsibilities, for tougher work and change.

Speaking to all the women recently, it was interesting to hear them discussing the notion of 'success' in these times of relative hardship. As you will see from the interviews, and from women like Tina Knight, many have already proclaimed the virtue of taking their business cautiously. On the whole, these women tend to be people who have *not* over-borrowed, nor over-extended, who are not pushing to be the biggest and brightest among their competitors. They admit to leaner times, to a tougher fight. Yet, as entrepreneurs, they seem genuinely quite confident. No entrepreneur takes her or his income for granted. They know each day counts for itself, that security will never come from outside sources and that they just have to keep up the momentum.

However, several women in the book do talk of the darker side of running a business: the secret that lies behind the risk-taker's door. There have been those moments of panic, particularly at 4 a.m., when they wake up and realize that they have burdened themselves with huge bank loans; they have talked backers into supporting them; they have acquired staff – and now it is up to them to live up to the potential. Hard times, in one sense, bring out the fighting spirit in the true entrepreneur. They are more taken aback when things go too easily.

When I considered whether there was a fairly typical attitude towards running a business which linked this group of women, two names immediately sprung to mind. They are more obvious names than others, being visible figures in the retail sector: Emma Bridgewater, of Bridgewater pottery and Prue Leith of Leith's restaurants and catering services (recently voted Business Woman of the Year in the Veuve Cliquot Awards). Either woman could by now have created retail outlets on every High Street in the country (following the path of the well-known giants of our times). Either woman could have sold franchises from her initial success. Both say that is not the way they envisage or even desire growth to take place.

An image was given to the nation during the past decade, not only of a powerful woman at the helm, but of the sense and sensibility that can lie behind such power. Its strength lies in what could be termed 'housewifely' knowledge: that there is no point in spending more than you have in your purse. It may be the kind of comment that leads certain women, and men, to cringe. Yet there is a truth behind it: women are used to budgeting, to making expenses meet; they tend not to be so foolish-headed, nor so feeble-minded, that they cannot handle finances. It is simply that, until very recently, women were never allowed the power or the freedom to exercise that talent.

Most encouragingly, the women interviewed here all seem to share an invaluable self-confidence. So, here is wishing luck to them, and to you, if you decide to start up or already are running your own business.

old notion

Part One

STARTING UP

Chapter One

THE START-UP:
LESSONS FROM THE
FRONT LINE

THE THREE FOLLOWING accounts which describe women's experiences, of setting up and running their own businesses, are not included as perfect examples of how to go about starting-up a business.

Each woman had been in business, at the time of our discussion, for between three and six years. Their stories reflect the variety of methods that may be employed in the process of plucking an initial idea or concept out of the air, placing it firmly on the ground, or launching it up into what one might hope is the sky.

Two of the stories involve manufacturing businesses, being run by women from very different social backgrounds, who approached their start-up from opposite ends of the spectrum. The third story is of a woman who took a small service industry, from being a one-woman freelance operator, to a company with six staff, prestigious offices and a client base that would make many larger companies suffer twinges of envy.

Just how did these women go about getting a business going? How easy was it to convince banks to lend them the money? How difficult was the process of hiring their own staff, getting their product into the shops or into the customer's home? How tricky was it to convince major clients that what they had to offer was what the client wanted to buy?

When it comes down to basics, the only attributes seemingly necessary for starting up a business are: bottomless supplies of energy, determination, enthusiasm, courage, gut instincts, perseverance, staying power, humour and the ability *not* to listen to negative opinions about your chances of survival and/or success. The blinkered approach in such cases has to be the best. The one vital ingredient underlying all the above is that of boundless reserves of self-confidence, which you may indeed not have at the outset. But, somewhere along the path to running your business, miraculously it is acquired.

Today newspapers

DOUNNE ALEXANDER-MOORE
Gramma's Original
Herbal Pepper Sauces

STARTING UP A business may come easily to some. But, probably for the vast majority of women, the mere thought of the financial and emotional risks involved, the banks and other officials to be dealt with, would be deterrent enough against moving forward, even if they were convinced their innovative idea was the best.

Dounne (pronounced Dawn), a Trinidadian-born British woman, who had a dream one day to launch hot pepper sauces on the unsuspecting British market (sauces based on recipes from her Caribbean herbalist grandmother), is remarkable in every facet. Dounne has taken her dream, within three years, from a position whereby she would boil up pans of peppers in her East End council flat kitchen, to one where she operates from a small factory and already supplies Tesco's, Sainsbury's and selected Safeway stores. She has done all this against every odd in the book.

Dounne's story is at once a hard-luck tale and an incredible paean to the spirit of survival; of true grit, determination and the pluck we know to be common among so many women (though it is not always followed through with such remarkable vengeance). Recently, Dounne was awarded the prestigious *Options* magazine award, sponsored by TSB Unit Trusts, as the best newcomer in the 'Women Mean Business' line-up. The competition is open to all women who run their own

7

businesses and each year the judges look for the most successful companies, that are being run with entrepreneurial flair and financial acumen. She is notably the first British black woman *ever* to have won a national business prize.

Lenny Henry launched the opening of her 1200 sq ft Essex-based factory unit in January 1990. From the very beginning, Dounne has shown a natural gift for publicizing Gramma's. She has also evinced a tremendous fighting spirit in the face of seemingly *insurmountable* obstacles along the way. In the words of her own press release, (written of course by herself) Dounne summed up her feats this way:

> She is a source of inspiration to others proving that although she is over forty years old, a woman, black, working class (living in a council flat), a single-parent (with two daughters of twenty-one and sixteen years), was on income support without money or collateral at the time of setting up the new business venture, she has still been able to accomplish all her dreams.

'Walking out on my husband was where my life started changing. It was a drastic step, but one that meant I was in fact saying: "Now I'm going to take charge of my life, I'll do what I want to do. Whether I make it or not, at least I'm going to have a go!"

'It was back in 1986, when I was thirty-eight years old that I took my two teenage daughters to live with me in a council flat, for the first time. I just knew I had to make a go of my own life. At the time, I had a job with a shipping company as a bookkeeper. Prior to that I had worked in housing management for thirteen years, and even before that as a laboratory technician for four years. On the business side, I had gathered some knowledge of management from bookkeeping and housing work, and of chemical testing from the laboratory. But I lacked any direct commercial experience.

'The idea of setting up my own business came from my daughters. I had always made the hot pepper sauces at home, and was well known for my unique cooking style – which was steeped in the Caribbean tradition, based on my grandmother's own herbal remedies. My daughters were fed up hearing me always complaining that I was broke. They persuaded me to go into business for myself.

'But I started absolutely from scratch. I had to choose the size of the jars, the packaging, design and write the labels, write and distribute my own press releases. I believed very strongly in the *quality* of my product and just prayed it would stand up for itself in the marketplace. At the very beginning, my goal was simply to get my product on the shelves of Harrods. I imagined it might take something like ten years. In fact it took me just three months!'

8

So how did Dounne promote her pepper sauces, from the backroom kitchen to Harrods, in seemingly such an easy and swift manoeuvre?

'I put together the first basic press release, determined to bring attention to my product. But the release itself was nothing special. I have had only a rudimentary education, nevertheless even I am appalled looking back to see the spelling mistakes!! I even spelled the word "goals" as "golds"! And, of course, I had no contacts in the media. But I just naively sent off the release to the features section editor, or in some cases the editor of different newspapers and magazines, telling them the history of my sauce and its health-giving values. Also I made it known that I intended to launch a nationwide educational campaign, on why the British people need to bring spicy foods into their diet.

'The media have, in fact, been wonderful to me. Never has anything negative been written. I have appeared in almost every form of media, with constant appearances. The *Observer* newspaper was the first to print the story, giving me a half-page, in which they described me, the sauces and my medicinal supportive evidence. I have appeared in most major newspapers, many local papers, on television programmes and on countless radio spots. Throughout the three years, I'd say hardly a month has gone by without some media attention. Of course it helps that I am a woman and that I am black. But I also benefit from having a unique product and an interesting story to tell.'

How Dounne went into production

'There I was, living in a council flat with my two daughters, a dog and a cat. Bear in mind that we are not allowed to use council-rented properties for commercial reasons. Only if you are doing market research are you able to make any kind of product. So I had to stick to that level of testing out the market, which meant everything was being sent out free to the Press.

'I had my small job, but even with that amount of pay I was receiving additional state support to help me keep the girls. When you are starting up a business, you cannot expect to make any money for the first two years; if you are lucky in that time even to get it off the ground. Indeed, you are most likely to make a massive loss. At a certain point you have to confront the fact you will need somehow to borrow money to buy stock, repay your debts, pay your staff, be able to sell your product, have enough money to restock. All this while *no* money is coming in. To make matters worse for me, living in the council property, I ran the risk of eviction. Hot pepper sauces are not something that can be made in secret. The smell is too strong!

'To get a new product on to the market is also very difficult, and I'm sure it is doubly so to begin the process as a black woman. But never once did I compromise my own goals. My aim was to get the product into the mainstream, to educate people, to sell the idea of "quality" and that this is an exceptional food product. In a sense, I was ahead of my time. What I am marketing is a health-based quality food product (I suppose the only equivalent would be the Body Shop's quality cosmetic products). Gramma's Herbal Pepper Sauce is a rich concentrated paste, a real product made with real food – not padded out with fillers.

'Word began to go around immediately. Very early on, two local television programmes, on rival channels, covered the sauce on the very *same* evening. I had targeted Harrods as a high-quality department store, which would not want to order in great quantities, and yet would not be put off by the expense. The price of Gramma's is way above that of mass-produced food products, but then the price is right for the quality of pure, concentrated foodstuff.

'My father took the jars himself into Harrods and Fortnum & Mason. It meant his lifelong dream had come true. Promotionally, I just seemed to know exactly what to do next, by instinct. The local television programmes filmed the first customers buying the sauce directly from Harrods' shelves. Can you imagine the uproar it caused being on those two spots together? Within three hours the next day, Harrods had sold 500 jars. That first week, they sold 1,000 jars, while we struggled to make enough to keep up the supply. I was still stirring the pots with a giant wooden spoon in my kitchen.

'While my sales were booming and we were still making all the sauces by hand, trying desperately not to annoy the neighbours (though I was ultimately reported to the council and threatened with eviction), it became obvious that I had to give up my job, to be able to supply enough jars to keep up with demand. You try and work it out: I was on Income Support and, of course, whilst receiving state benefit you are not allowed to work more than twenty-four hours in a week. I had to pretend not to be working, that this was only "market research". But also, somehow, I had to raise some finance. If you are on Income Support you cannot raise capital. No bank would look at the work I had already achieved. Bank managers only wanted to know where my collateral was coming from.'

Dounne is still bitter about the attitude she met from banks and about all the advertising hype that surrounds the so-called government enterprise schemes for small businesses. The path to any such forms of help, as she well knows, is loaded with land mines.

'To begin with, no bank would see me as anything other than a black woman, which, to them, meant that I would only ever be in a position to market to other black people. They could not see me selling Gramma's into the mainstream of British society. Then, double this immediate negative image with the fact that I am a woman, and you find that banks trivialize your ideas. As a woman, I have learned the hard way that you have to be able to sell yourself. All the input, the energy, the self-confidence, has to come from your own initiative.

'To this day, I believe that banks are more likely to lend money to a woman if there is a man behind you. To be a woman on your own is to invite suspicion. And worse, if you are a single parent, then you are assumed to be unstable. However, should you once find a good bank manager, then my advice is to grab him and keep him! Alternatively, if you come across bad ones, then move on. A bad bank manager will not improve over time in his attitude. He may be deep down jealous. Yet at the same time, he knows that he has the controlling power and just may use that vindictively. Only recently, for example, despite my proven success, I was told by a bank manager that I should have stayed in my kitchen and remained small. "It's only a jar of pickle", were his words.

'One aspect I would emphasize to women contemplating starting a business: you will have to be strong enough to face that kind of negative response, to be able to pick yourself up and try again until you succeed. It is never easy to be your own boss, yet somehow women like myself are propelled along, refusing to give up. Never did I realize that I was such a fighter, nor how strong I could be!

'For two years, I approached banks, but as I had no personal finance or collateral nothing moved. My husband had sold off our former house and had given me £15,000 as my share. But that had already been absorbed by the business. The banks continued to turn me down, despite all my promotional abilities, because I had no financial backing. I was also told that I was too ambitious, because I had asked for a minimum of a £50,000 loan to set up. But then, as even my faith was beginning to diminish, I found a young bank manager who was wonderful and who was prepared to help me.'

Ultimately, Dounne was backed by the Government Small Firms Loan Guarantee scheme, whereby the Government acts as guarantor on the loan. Yet she is hardly enthusiastic about the system and its practices.

'The whole scheme is a farce. Neither the banks nor probably the Government themselves understand the way businesses work. As I see it, millions of pounds are poured into these regional initiatives,

11

but the money is all recycled back into the system, spent on their own advertising, office rents and the staff wages; the money does not go to the people who need it most. So, when the Government brags and claims they have spent £9 billion on these schemes, you can rest assured the money goes round in circles among themselves. It most certainly is not going to *people* running small businesses, who are only entitled to free advice.

'Supposedly, banks are enabled to lend money to someone like me – a man or woman with no income or collateral, who has developed a business and can go no further unless they can expand – up to a maximum of £100,000. But most banks, I have discovered, won't make use of the scheme, because either they do not understand it, or they have never had to put it into practice. It was up to me to confront the bank with the information.

'In the last year, when so many businesses have gone under because of high interest rates, you might be interested to know that what appears to be so generous – the Small Firms Loan Guarantee Scheme – is in fact another disaster. On the scheme, we have to pay 2 per cent above bank interest rates. How can a small start-up business afford such a rate? Of the £100,000 I eventually managed to borrow, during the past year £35,000 went straight back to the bank in interest. In fact, it has cost me £110,000 just to set up, without even thinking about wages, raw materials or running costs such as the telephone, gas and lights. All the investment has gone on the factory unit, equipment and paying interest.

'The people who administer the finance in banks have, for the most part, never run a business themselves. Even many of the experts at the Enterprise Agencies tend to be inexperienced people advising the even more inexperienced. As a direct result of my experience, once a month I myself give lectures through a local Enterprise Agency to ordinary people wanting to set up a business: giving them the facts and an idea of what it really takes; how much strength and commitment they will actually need.

'It is one hard slog! What I tell them is that I may have been to hell and back. But . . . I'm nearing success. I also explain that you may be taught the basics of bookkeeping and administration, but no-one can really teach you *business*. That has to come from personal gut reaction or instinct.'

Recently, Dounne became so incensed by the continuing lack of support from her bank manager that she circulated a very effective press release to government departments and the media, outlining the problems she sees affecting small businesses. 'How and why the system is failing us,' she wrote in heartfelt anger. Showing her natural ability towards PR, she spelled out her message in a thought-provoking press release entitled The Black Cinderella:

Limited Finance
Limited Advice
Limited Back-up
Limited Support
Limited Time
No wonder they get Limited Business Success . . .

Business men or women like herself are trapped into paying the extremely high interest rates which in itself could drive them under.

Even though I've personally negotiated and obtained orders from Tesco's and Sainsbury's
Even though my business would create a unique and exclusive industry for Britain
Even though my business could create hundreds of jobs
Even though my business has colossal worldwide potential
Even though my business could increase Britain's exports
Even though my products could improve the nation's health
Even though my business supports many charities; other British businesses; the Third World and the Environment
Even though I've brought national recognition to Black British foods
Even though my business could enhance racial harmony
Even though my business offers real inspiration to others
My Bank Manager remains adamantly non-supportive and no-one will release me from the noose of the Government Small Firms Loan Guarantee Scheme. Why do they bother to encourage New Enterprise or Initiatives?

The main advice she has received from the bank has been along the following lines: that she should take her products to a large food manufacturer like Crosse & Blackwell and pay them to take on its production. Indeed, she comments, the last piece of advice was that she should seek legal help for the possibility of liquidation as the bank may at any time demand full repayment of the loan!

Hard words for a woman who is nevertheless undaunted and determined to survive. Her document was at the time of our speaking already attracting interest from various bodies concerned with encouraging small businesses.

*

But then Dounne's greatest achievements have indeed come about from her own instincts; her sheer uncanny sense of how to attract business and make sales. The design of her packaging, logos, the jars themselves, any promotional plans, all have come from her. She relies on her elder daughter for help with correspondence, bookkeeping, office procedures and the VAT work. Her mother helps with making the sauces; her father still handles some of the distribution. Her brother-in-law is the financial adviser. Costs have to be kept to a minimum when, as she says, your main expense in the first two years is equipment, to enable you to develop the product.

To print press releases and any corporate design, she has not strayed beyond a local Prontaprint shop in Barking, Essex, where she has developed a healthy working relationship with the owner and staff of the franchise. Currently her greatest achievement is that she has been recognized by the supermarket chains, an almost unheard of feat: Tesco's, Sainsbury's and Safeway's stores have taken on Gramma's, a small new product, and given it a major launch. By December 1991, she promises Gramma's will be in 1,000 stores across the UK.

Let me creep, before I walk

'A lot of new products are rejected weekly by supermarkets. One buyer told me that he was turning down large established companies who were spending £2 – £4 million on advertising, so small businesses don't have a chance of getting in unless they had an exceptional product. Again, I have been very very fortunate. Tesco's is putting Gramma's into 150 Superstores, while Safeway's are placing it in 300 stores. My product is being tested in the market for Sainsbury's; and many others are also interested.

'How did I go about approaching the supermarkets? I just thought about it. My strategies miraculously always seemed to be right. For Tesco's, I found the name of the main grocery buyer and wrote him a letter, which I followed up with a phone call two weeks later. They said "Yes" straight away. I made it to the two top supermarket chains right from the beginning! By this time, I very much needed supermarket support and interest because, with the running costs of the factory unit, I found myself no longer able to afford to distribute my goods to smaller stores. Tesco's come by with their own trucks to pick up from my unit.

'My way of dealing with what is certainly new pressure has never been to hide the fact that I am small, or where I'm coming from, in the face of these giants. Tesco's have been excellent in offering advice. They care, they really do. They have admitted to me that they're taking a risk, because my business is so small. But I asked them not to force me immediately into huge expansion. I want to

14

creep before I learn to walk. So it was my suggestion that we limit the test run to their Superstores, as I could not at the time handle supplying to all the stores.

'My ultimate goal now is to establish a major manufacturing plant somewhere in the United Kingdom.

'All along, I knew the potential was there. Working from my kitchen I had already established a good mail order business around the world. The letters of testimonial that come in are still quite incredible. My customers even then were from a variety of countries and backgrounds. And, interestingly, they were mostly white people who were discovering that my claims were true: my herbal pepper sauces are beneficial to your health. I also received medical back-up, from Dr Irwin Ziment, a British professor working in America, who believes implicitly that the white people need more spicy food in their diet.'

Dounne has now established the first product range of Gramma's concentrated herbal pepper sauces (mild, hot, extra-hot and super-hot), which are the original ancient Hot Herbal Sauces. Twenty or so other natural food products are ready to be developed. She claims that most British people believe spicy food to be indigestible, because they assume that black and white peppercorns, and mustard, are integral to spices – but these are the culprits leading to stomach problems. Her sauces include digestible herbs and spices, which help to purify the blood, improve circulation, and are excellent for respiratory disorders such as emphysema, bronchitis and asthma; they are also highly beneficial in today's polluted environment and for smokers and 'flu sufferers.

What ideas for the future?

'My potential market in America could be huge. So I am waiting for another year until I'm good and ready to take that on, because I have to be capable of turning over 100,000 jars a week to export there. I know that promotionally my possibilities are endless, in the States. Over there, they will be fascinated by the idea of a black woman from Britain running her own successful business, and they will love the pepper sauces.

'My recipes are based on common everyday knowledge from over 100 years ago in Trinidad. I sincerely believe I have the capacity to change round the entire health foods' market, selling these products to ordinary people at a price they can afford.

'Women have always been natural fighters. We just don't always realize our own strengths. I have been through a lot of bad experiences in starting up, especially at the beginning when I lacked confidence. But I have learned to take the negatives and to make something positive

15

out of them. Finding myself on my own, with two daughters to raise, was incentive enough. You learn in business that the old adage, that life is very much what *you* make it, is so true. But, if I can make it, then so can anyone. If you have a dream, then it is up to you to turn it into a reality. No-one else will do that for you.'

Facts:
Staff: 5 family members.
Turnover: Gramma's expects to turnover £500,000 by 1991, after three years in business.

Harry Cory-Wright

EMMA BRIDGEWATER
Bridgewater pottery
and ceramics

TODAY, AT THE remarkably young age of twenty-nine, already having been in business for six years, Emma Bridgewater's tale of how she set up and so successfully launched her own company, is no less inspirational than Dounne's for the courage and daring she has displayed.

From an entrepreneurial background, with a father in business, Emma went to London University to read English. But, even on graduation, she knew she wanted to run her own business. What she eventually launched was a business whereby she designs and manufactures spongeware pottery, based on late eighteenth-century practices. But, most intriguingly, Emma had no formal training in art, design or business.

The business has moved from strength to strength. Recently, she opened her first shop in Fulham, which has a wonderfully historical feel to its cosy crowded dressers and tables, literally groaning with the uniquely decorated jugs, cups, plates and bowls.

Emma is married to Matthew Rice, formerly a partner in Viscount Linley's furniture making company. He runs his own business, Rice Paper, concentrating on decorative stationery. To add to her credits, Emma juggles motherhood with running the business. At the time of our meeting, their daughter was eighteen months old and she was well into her second pregnancy (her second daughter was born in mid-January). Emma is tall, striking looking, forceful in character and a 100 per cent determined businesswoman.

What made Emma decide from such a young age to set up her own business?

'My father was in business and instinctively I found that I understood just how much leeway such independence can give you. I suppose that appealed to me from the very beginning. Also, I found that handling a turnover was fascinating, compared to dealing, for example, with a very limited salary. But I would say it goes back to the fact I had absolutely no idea what I wanted to do after university. I was typical of the millions of girls who go through school, doing Arts subjects, keeping their options open until something reveals itself.

'Immediately after university, I fell into an interesting job working for Sally Muir's and Joanna Osborne's Warm and Wonderful Knitwear company. Business was booming for them and I became involved in recruiting up to 800 home knitters. It was a small company, run by women, which was informal enough in its set-up to allow me to see exactly what was going on. A lot of the theories I'd learned from my father I could then see being put into practice. During that time, I managed to save a few hundred pounds, knowing only that I wanted to set up my own business, but not what that business would be. Although I did know it would not be making jumpers!

'I realized that the reason Sally and Joanna were successful was essentially that they were servicing their own kind. That made me look around at what I, and my circle of friends, might want to *buy*. I had done some odd jobs cooking and looking after children, through which it struck me that what was missing was contemporary earthenware. Everything we were using at home, for example, was nineteenth century. Any contemporary earthenware currently on the market, we wouldn't dream of buying because it was remarkably unpleasant.

'Another gut instinct was to know that I did not want to spend a hundred years setting up the production processes myself. This was something I had learned from working with the knitters: to go into business I should tap into the manufacturing process. It would have been the kiss of death to have begun by turning out a few nice pots myself, because there is an obvious limit to the numbers you can make. I wanted to find an industrial context which I could slightly manipulate.

'The whole point about marketing goods I already knew: what makes a piece of pottery worth £7.99 rather than 99p is all in the *design*. The basic cost need hardly change. My plan was to find a factory which would make the initial shape, on to which I would add my own spongeware designs. The main problems along the way were firstly to find someone prepared to make such a small quantity on my behalf; and secondly that I did not like any of the shapes that were being produced. I was, therefore, forced to design my own range of shapes too.'

How did Emma go about finding a factory?

'That was down to luck, in the end. A graphic designer friend suggested a factory in Stoke-on-Trent where they were mostly making ashtrays for pubs. The point about this particular factory is that the owner concentrates on making a very good quality product. His standards are high which is sadly unusual in Stoke these days. He was also hungry enough to take on such a hare-brained scheme as mine, and was interested in helping to create this new product. No-one else I approached was at all helpful.

'But I did have to approach the manufacturer from a very strange basis as I had absolutely no formal design training. All I had was an *idea* and a *desire* to make it work. I certainly did not come to him with a worked-out plan, which ultimately was an advantage as it meant that we could develop the ideas together, which led to his becoming equally involved. Many men in business would find that far too emotive a situation; it's not a way they would like to work. I've found that in describing the situation to male colleagues, they are horrified by the precariousness of the situation: for example, that I only have one supplier. At times, I must admit to finding it stressful. But then we do have a healthy working relationship. In many ways it has become as much his baby as mine. We both *have* to make it work.'

Did Emma approach the factory owner, or the bank, with a professional business plan?

'No, absolutely nothing like that. I had saved a little money with my bank, and they were used to me as a student being overdrawn. They just simply let me get away with borrowing, assuming I would repay the overdraft. I had been left a small amount of money by my grandmother which also helped. But, if I had had to draw up a business plan at the beginning to satisfy either a bank or an accountant, I would not be here now. I would probably have become a literary agent's assistant or something. I went into debt with the bank based purely on a hunch. I was sure; 100 per cent convinced. But no-one else would have been.

'One has to be monumentally fierce and determined, which can be hard for women, who tend to be naturally more honest and reticent. Men, I think, are better at blustering, at building up business plans.

21

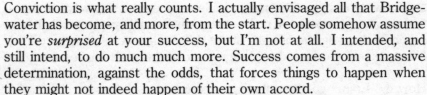

Conviction is what really counts. I actually envisaged all that Bridge-water has become, and more, from the start. People somehow assume you're *surprised* at your success, but I'm not at all. I intended, and still intend, to do much much more. Success comes from a massive determination, against the odds, that forces things to happen when they might not indeed happen of their own accord.

'I just knew that what I was going to make would be what people wanted to buy! That level of determination is actually very persuasive. There was never a moment that I was remotely tentative about my plans. Though, at first, when I was not making any money, I did go into a state of panic and took several boxes worth of pieces to Jubilee Market in Covent Garden. They were four very black Sundays, when I did not even cover the cost of the market stall (which was only sixteen pounds). But, I did meet three people at the market who turned out to be vital early stockists.'

How did Emma launch her pottery business?

'I was hell bent on getting out of the position of knocking on doors and into a state whereby I would carry my reputation with me. The very first thing I did, with my earliest samples, was to have them photographed, put together a press release, and pushed myself out there talking about the products. It was all in order to capture the attention of the buyers from Harrods and Harvey Nichols, for example, so they could give me a feeling of what they were look-ing for. I offered quite a wide selection, looking back it was far too many samples. I started with something like forty items which was bad news from the production point of view. But I sensed that the best way was to be flexible, and make myself able to pro-vide what they asked for. At the very last moment, that first year of starting out, I was told about the Top Drawer Gift Exhibition, which proved helpful in bringing me my first client, London's General Trading Company.'

Did she make the sales pitch completely cold?

'Although I knew that my intention was to do as little cold-calling as possible, at first I had to contact the buyers at the major department stores. They had been sent the snazzy-looking press release in ad-vance. I just would not turn up with a tatty suitcase of goods. It had to look more secure and more fun than that. I pitched my goods at a certain level even to the buyers. It was a very exciting time, with lots of ideas pouring out.

'From then on, I have pitched my marketing the right way round. I have been in the position of being able to offer something people want. Even the store buyers now come to me. They're happier that way, and so am I. You have to make it clear from the start that you can offer a good service.'

But does not a major store like Harrods only buy in certain quantities?

'No, one of the tricks is to set up with the viewpoint of finding what it is they want, and then being prepared to be flexible.

'Another virtue I had was that because of the factory and production costs, my spongeware arrived at the store at a reasonably high price. By the time the store's mark-up is added, the products had placed themselves naturally at the right end of the right market; for upmarket, discerning people, who don't mind paying extra for good traditional, high quality, durable goods. It also meant I was taken more seriously. If I had produced more cheaply, I would have been flooded with orders which probably we would not have been able to meet. Even as it is, we have gone through incredible gyrations, accommodating our growth within the confines of this one factory.'

How the relationship with the factory has worked
'There are many luck factors, things that have happened for which I cannot lay claim. For the last thirty years, Stoke-on-Trent has been in the industrial doldrums, for example, with terrible destructive takeovers whereby a lot of the smaller companies have lost out. None of the big companies I broached were interested in design. No-one out there was taking an innovative risk. The skills in the workforce are available, but they are fast diminishing.

'For about two months, I did try to do my own decorating. I would rush up to Stoke, and stay for a few days to demonstrate what I had in mind to the workers. But the plan was that the factory girls would take over the spongeing. It is in fact a very straightforward technique, but it requires considerable dexterity. For a time, I had fantasized that I could contract the decorating out to a handicapped workshop. But I'm afraid I had to shelve that idea, as I was just giving myself too many problems.

'I am actually constantly aware that it is to my advantage that I do not have an art school training. It means I am not bringing what would seem to be inflammatory foreknowledge, to what is already a very stressful situation, when negotiating a contract with the factory owner which he could see as threatening. I approach the work more at the factory's level. I do not try to make things happen that they cannot accommodate.'

*

Can Emma explain why her relationship with the factory has been so successful?

'In a way, maybe it's simply because, for whatever reason, I have been producing what is fairly unique and is what people genuinely love to buy. I'm based in London and fundamentally am interested in what the shops want and how their selling procedures work; I'm aware of new designs around. Therefore I have a proper grasp of what we're trying to make, and why we want to produce it.

'I spend a considerable time up in Stoke, dividing my days between the factory and the warehouse; learning how the factory works and how we can adapt ourselves to suit their imponderables; persuading them slowly to bring about changes at their end. Curiously, large companies like Marks and Spencer, and Laura Ashley, don't invest in such a level of research. They appear to take no trouble to understand the manufacturing process, and they certainly never innovate, but merely adapt what is available.

'Our stated aim, however, is to investigate the ways in which companies worked – those who have traditionally decorated earthenware – which explains the wonderful power and strength of the Staffordshire potteries in the eighteenth century. Also we wanted to discover where a lot of that talent still lies, and to achieve a similar level of quality. It requires a degree of sensitivity to work alongside a factory and its workers in this way. No-one else seems to do such groundwork.

'Basically, as I see it, there is a total lack of interest from the South East, the middle classes, the university educated classes, in the process of *manufacturing*. Too often, design and marketing skills are to be found in these classes. But the other form of brilliance that goes into *making* the actual goods is separated from them by a terrible chasm.'

If she plans to expand, how will Emma move beyond the manufacturing capability of this one factory? Would she seek factories abroad?

'It is tempting! We have just returned from New York where we were comparing the market. Their department store buyers import from Italy. Those buyers are a whole new breed: much more innovative, demanding, and stylish than you find here. All the top stores have done very impressive work with Italian potteries. But that would prove a problem for me, in that I see myself working very much within the English tradition, which becomes slightly nonsensical if I apply that to an Italian object. Their quality is rather different, too. It's rough, the product of a very different culture: cheap and disposable, would not withstand the dishwasher, rather coarse and hefty earthenware.

24

Whereas mine is at once more refined but will last 100 years. Besides, I would not want to make a mongrel, half-Italian and half-English.'

Because they already export to America, Japan, Australia, and more recently to Europe, I was intrigued by how Emma had set about learning all the different stages of moving into different markets?

'Probably the best thing about gaining a university degree is that, within the principle of writing an essay, you learn all the basic elements of researching. One piece of advice my father gave me early on was that whatever you want to know you can find out, but don't squander your chances of asking. Be straightforward. If you know what you're asking for people will be very helpful. So I always just turn to people for help, until I reach the point where I can go it alone.

'We have learned to tackle the export market by looking for a sympathetic organization on the other side – similar businesses to our own working on a small, human scale – who understand what we are about. For example, in America, we found a distributor for Matthew's stationery. They have done such a great job getting us into the stores, and they are so highly motivated, that now we have been having discussions with them to expand and take on distribution of the pottery too. It is solutions like that, that we look for.'

Will there be a Bridgewater on every High Street?

So now to the important question. How big does Emma intend the business to grow. Already she has a staff of ten in the London base, and four or five more working in Stoke. But does she fantasize about becoming as big as Laura Ashley, for example? Does she want to see her own shops in every town centre?

'I don't know, I don't think so. Of course it would be wonderful to succeed to that extent, but I have mixed feelings about going public, raising so much capital for expansion. It's too risky. Once you go into public ownership, creativity seems to become more or less exhausted. Creativity and innovation are innately expensive aspects, like a bottomless pit. Right now we have only one shop in London and we supply independent and department stores. We sell in an *ad hoc* way to all comers. Yet this way, we maintain control of quality.

'We are looking to expand into home furnishings, textiles and carpets, but we have to gauge how far to go. Timing that kind of expansion and getting it right is crucial. One avenue we are exploring is that of setting up small boutiques in the larger stores. I haven't yet cracked the problem. It means working out exactly what sort of environment

Bridgewater fits, and adapting that for a set-up in a small craft shop or a huge store.

'Times, as we all know, are tough, but so far we are having a miraculously unstressful time. Ordering is as strong as ever. I do not foresee a profound negative change. In fact it is a very interesting time, just like the beginning of the Eighties. Many businesses will go down, but others will replace them. Already, I have made changes because of the way we have grown. For example, I am no longer Managing Director, but Chairman. We brought in Marcus Pollen, from his sister Arabella Pollen's company, to be MD. Marcus brings with him a whole chunk of cool, calm, collected financial acumen.

And for the future, what does she see for herself?

'Oh, moving into other careers as well as the pottery. I've always loved education, and book publishing. I have a terrible restless insanity. Right now, with one daughter and a second on the way I do find "running a shop" quite limiting. I don't really want to be doing this full time for the rest of my life. Many women must find the same: that it's one thing to be running a business when you're single, but quite different when you're married, and different again when you have a family.'

How do family and business fit together?

'Well, it's not quite the flexible situation I might have imagined. More likely is the comparison that it's as though you already have a family of handicapped children, and now you're having another child. To be good at business you have to give it your first loyalty. Someone has to be around to stay up all night if a problem arises. That is why I stopped being MD. There came a point when I asked myself was someone else going to raise my child for me? If not, I had to arrange more time for myself.

'I always have to clock-watch. We have a live-in nanny. But I tend to work from 9 a.m. to 6 p.m., and won't stay late very often. Of course, I can take time off in the day if I need to. Right now, I worry about combining the stress of business and having a family. Partly, I feel it might come from trying to run things in an amateurish way. It has come to a question of hiring more professional staff and of delegating further. My father believes I should take time out now to go to London Business School, or somewhere of that kind, for some real management training. We probably need more sophisticated management methods here.

'I do have to control my working day, but one advantage is that we live 50 yards away. So, at lunchtimes as a family we can meet together. About once a week all the company meets for lunch. That's a nice precedent of the ideal way I see working life operating. I believe in

26

keeping reasonably small. What tends to happen to people is that they grow a smallish high-quality business, then at the right time sell out and it becomes a High Street chain – no longer committed to quality.'

Will she be taking much time off for the new baby?

'I hope so, I didn't take enough off for my first daughter. Although in the heat of that summer, I more or less gave up in the last six weeks, still I was at work until the end. Then, after she was born, I couldn't resist coming in two days later. Not to sit at my desk, but just to oversee things. That's why I say it is so difficult to combine business and family. I cannot simply say I'll stop now and disappear for three to six months.

'Besides, I have no idea how easy this next baby will be. Some newborns keep you up all night and then you really cannot devote much energy to work. Obviously, for me I can write in a certain amount of flexibility to my life. I certainly don't have to set off at 7 a.m. with my briefcase, and be gone for the whole day! I would say I am getting close to a reasonable way of life by now.'

Facts:
Staff: At present 14 in London, and another 4 or 5 in Stoke-on-Trent.
Turnover: Although they do not bandy figures around because, when a company is relatively new, those figures might sound surprisingly high or low, Emma estimates this year will be around £1,500,000.

PENNY PHIPPS
Phipps Public Relations Ltd

FOR MANY WOMEN, one obvious incentive to starting up their own business is the arrival of a child, and the ensuing realization that they no longer want to commit themselves to a full-time out-of-the-home working life. The temptation then is to turn freelance, continue with their chosen profession, working perhaps in a less pressured way based from home; or to share the cost of office space with a few associates.

Public relations has long been a traditionally female industry. It is one of the service industries that seems to have an in-built female appeal and structure; and one that has attracted many to arrange it on a small 'suits me' basis from their homes. What is interesting then, in the scope of this book, is to meet a woman who followed that path at first, but who then decided to branch out from the 'small is nice and comfortable', to set up a major PR firm based on her own name and reputation.

The story of Penny Phipps is all the more intriguing because she began in that traditional way. She made an enormous leap to turn her one-woman freelance band into a sound, solid, bona-fide business, now a member of the Public Relations Consultants Association.

Unlike the two women previously described in this section, Penny went about the start-up of her new business in a formal way. Having graduated from Sussex University with an English degree, she moved into professional PR, working for a stream of publishers. But, apart from the normal professional involvement, she had no business knowledge. Penny took herself back to college to learn precisely how to set up a business. She plunged in the determined way, taking out a sizeable loan from the bank, finding premises and hiring staff.

Phipps PR is now a full-service public relations consultancy with a thoroughly thought-out concept of business and quality of service. Notably, all members of staff work as a team on an equal level as senior members with expertise. There are no secretaries but there are administrative and bookkeeping support staff.

Clients include publishing companies and authors, celebrities, design companies such as David Linley's furniture business, environmental agencies and concerns, food, wine and spirits companies, health associations, leisure groups, television companies, travel groups and the recently launched distance-learning programme for Small Businesses put together by Cranfield School of Management, in conjunction with the Open University and the BBC.

Penny herself is a delightful and charming woman. Now thirty-nine, she does not fit any preconceived image of the self-made business woman. Her company operates from well-appointed offices in Central London, close to Bloomsbury. I asked Penny why she felt so many women wanted to run their own businesses?

'In my case it was being twenty-seven, having a baby, and wondering if I could possibly return to my full-time job. I had been in book publishing PR since university, concentrating on author book launch tours. But very quickly on returning to work I realized that I just was not seeing enough of my son. I thought about getting a part-time job, but there really were not any available. This was twelve years ago, when it was not possible to negotiate such terms with an employer. All the time though, I knew that I did not want to be at home permanently, without a job.

'Then one day I just said to myself, "Why not run your own business?" It seemed a good idea! But, how to do it was the worry. It was the time of Shirley Conran's *Superwoman*, and one phrase from her book inspired me: something along the lines of "Stop sitting around thinking about things, worrying whether you can do them, just get on and do it!" I said to myself, "Why not? The only way to start is to do it."

'The publishers I had been working for, Hutchinson's and Macdonald's for example, always had a lot of seasonal work when they needed extra staff. So to begin with, I offered them my services on a freelance basis and, indeed, they were downright grateful as it meant they could hire me for a project, or to take over an author tour, without increasing their staffing load. And that was how I started out, very much as a freelancer with no overheads. At first I based myself from home, or I would work in their offices, using their phones and support services, for specific projects. Eventually, I took a desk in someone else's Covent Garden office, which gave me a business address and meant that I could invest in impressive stationery. But still I was seeing myself very much as "just a freelancer".'

How does one make the move from being a freelancer to becoming a real business?

'If ten years ago I had said to myself, "I'm going to start up a business, find offices and employ my own staff," I doubt anything would have happened. The very thought would have been too much. Maybe I would never have achieved all this, had I thought too heavily about the consequences. In some ways naïvety and ignorance are helpful: I had not reached that level of management in my own working life and knew nothing, for example, about budgeting and finance; nothing about how to set up a business.

'But, three years ago, I changed my way of thinking about my new working life: that it was all very well to know how to do PR, which was my profession. I could bring in enough work to pay myself, and maybe one or two others, if I needed help. But there is a lot more to running a business than that, especially if you intend to grow. To take the next step, there are certain basics that I now know you have to understand. This may mean how to negotiate with the bank manager; or even to appreciate that you *can* bargain with him (or her) and that if you are displeased it's all right to take your custom elsewhere.

'That was why I went to business school: to learn everything there is to know about starting up a small business. Initially, I had contemplated taking an MBA, but that would have been too time-consuming, and the courses are really aimed at those people planning to find work with the big corporations. So it took a blinding flash of inspiration even for me to think of doing a course on "small businesses"! Such courses are not very well known and, to make matters worse, it takes quite an effort to track down where they might be available. Up-to-date information should be available from the Training Agency, Moorfoot, Sheffield, as things have changed since my own course. But my advice would still be: keep looking, courses do exist. I was very lucky to be offered a place on Cranfield School of Management's course. It involved a stiff entry test, as they wanted to be sure that the business you were setting up would, with the result of their training, grow and ultimately employ more people. They prefer to take on businesses that have already been running for 1–2 years. They have found that, within a year of the course, businesses tend to flourish. The main reason for that I am sure is that they give these new business owners much more self-confidence in taking decisions.

'The course was, however, extremely beneficial. One weekend a month, I would attend a full-time intensive residential session. We were set homework and, most constructively, had a permanent counsellor. I still keep in touch with my counsellor, for example. While I was taking the course, I was actually starting up the business proper. In fact, as working on the business plan is a major part of your work at Cranfield, which should in theory take up to six months to complete, I had to speed up the process as raising money for the expansion was my primary goal.'

But what fundamental help could such a course offer? Were there not elements that even common sense could have supplied?

'I was moving from being a freelancer, and intending to change and develop the scope of my work from my background in publishing PR. My colleague of several years, Miranda Page-Wood, was joining me in the business as a director and shareholder. I sensed that between us we had other skills that could be developed to move into more commercial and industrial forms of PR. But we needed to know how to market ourselves, how to understand the books, and how to create a good balance between finding new and running current projects.

'Basically, as far as the finance side goes, as a housewife I knew you had to bring in more money than you spend. But I really did not want to continue allowing bank managers and accountants to show me lists of figures without my understanding. I would look at the figures in brackets, for example, and say in bewilderment, "What are those?" They would reply, "Oh, don't you worry about that. We'll sort it out." I had reached the point of thinking, "No, I want to *know*. I'm the one taking the risk. I want to see those figures every month and remain on top of the situation."

'In fact, once I took up the studies, I became totally absorbed in my new learning, and hooked on reading business books! Even now, I find it makes the business more fun if I really understand what is going on. If we are having a bad month, at least I have ideas of what can be done.'

The isolation factor

'The other incentive for taking the course is the fact it is very lonely running your own business. My husband did not want me coming home every evening, going on about my problems. I needed permanent advisers, people who would not raise their eyebrows and groan to talk over one more time issues relating to Phipps PR! This was a major breakthrough in my thinking, adopted from the course. I changed the business from being that of a sole trader, to becoming a limited company, with a board of directors and two non-executive directors, who were to be my seniors, who would look over the figures at board meetings, and if necessary who would shout at me, and keep me on my toes. It really does work like that. The non-executive directors will criticize the way we operate. I'm prepared to listen to them and not to be upset, but to accept their advice as mentors.

'I was very lucky in being able to attract Dr Miriam Stoppard as one non-executive director. We had known each other for several years, through publishing, and she is very interested in new businesses. She also has tremendous energy, is full of ideas and totally understands the financial implications. Our other non-executive director is Robin Kinnear, who set up his own PR company Kinnear Ltd, five years ago. He is much further down the track than myself, brings in fee income of over £1 million a year and has a staff of about thirty. He is very much a mentor who can say to me, "I was at that stage three years ago," and then give me seasoned advice.'

First-class people hire first-class staff

'Robin's major piece of advice to me was on this level. He pointed out that as I was selling time and services to clients, I should have a really good team. One very basic lesson to take on board for a small business is that it is no good thinking, "I can't afford to hire people who expect good salaries." You *have* to go out to hire the very best you can afford, because these people are the sum of what you have to sell. That is why we have minimum support staff and no account handlers who're not top fee earners. Instead of directors with secretaries we now have a team of senior people with very different expertise, from varied backgrounds such as advertising or someone from a major corporate PR firm. They bring with them track record, reputation and terrific levels of expertise that I just don't have. With hindsight, it now seems an obvious ploy. But at the time it did not.

'It may be something of a cliché in the business world to talk about top-class people employing others even better than themselves. But it is an important concept. If you are really serious about your business, you will look to surround yourself with people, not to compliment you, or to remain in your shadow, but those who may outshine and will certainly drive you on. They should not be people whom you can squash. Personally, I have found it a great relief to delegate in this way. It can become a terrible responsibility being the boss; meaning you end up having even less time for yourself. To many, such delegation might be the hardest part of setting up a business: the moment you let others go with their own ideas, you have not got total control, and yet, of course, you are still left to worry about the expense.'

How did the expansion happen, the bank loan and the move to smart new offices?

'I went from a one-room shared office in Covent Garden, to three rooms in Soho, and then to our present offices which is a suite with a fairly prestigious address (and in reality is a much more pleasant working environment than we might have hoped for, being in a paved mews street, surrounded by restaurants and similar small companies). Before taking on the lease, I had only ever rented as a licensee. So, here again is the big change. Once you take on a major lease, you are in effect saying that you are in business; you are going to raise the money to pay for the lease, equip the office and hire the staff.

'As I mentioned, I had created a business plan and began to see bank managers with a request to borrow £50,000. The money was needed to cover the lease, the move, putting in computers, fax, phone lines, carpets, decent furniture. And it was to employ people on decent salaries. At first, there were just three of us rattling around in all the space. But I knew we were going to expand and, in fact, not long ago I took on further borrowing to acquire the lease for the upstairs floor as well. Right now we have it rented out, but when we reach the point of further expansion as I plan, then we will have the space.

'But I cannot say that arranging the borrowing was easy. Before I succeeded, I had to change banks a few times. In the end, I did find a great manager with whom I negotiated good terms on a loan and an overdraft facility. Most importantly, he did not insist I sign up our family home as collateral. All along, I refused to do that, as I could not live with such an element of risk. The loan was, therefore, unsecured. Whether that would be possible in today's more unhealthy economic climate, I am not sure; but the new manager was impressed by our team of seniors and also that we had begun already to attract some big clients.

'I needed a bank manager who would work with me, who would be prepared to offer advice. He was very clear from the outset, about why he has to be so cautious. The bank will only ever receive its set amount of interest. We, as the business partners, stand to make the profit, and in so doing we have to take the risk. If I wanted more financiers with a greater risk involvement, I would have to go to venture capitalists.'

Attracting the first 'big name' clients
'That was my very first step, to retain our publishing clients, but also to move on and develop our markets. Another mistake, I now realize,

34

that small companies make is to think that they are "little", so they can only work for other little companies. It all comes down to a question of a change in self-concept and self-promotion. Now we have made the leap, we find that many larger companies have, indeed, grown dissatisfied with big corporate PR firms, because they may have had the initial briefing meetings with a senior account executive, but then discovered that the real work was passed down to a junior. We now find ourselves in the fortunate position of working for a wide variety of clients and businesses. The clients are pleased with us and we, of course, are delighted.

'Our success is in having transformed ourselves from two or three people working within one industry, to a level where now we have six full-time PR executives, plus a couple of other staff on the financial side, working on a mixed portfolio of clients. I would plan to expand to about fifteen staff: that would be the right critical mass to enable us to bring in the volume of work.

'But, I will confess that it has involved a lot of risk. Nine months ago, there were times it felt as though I was standing on the window-sill out there, with nothing below me but a massive chasm of debt!'

Cash flow – the dreaded words for any new business

'With that level of debt there below us, I was very worried that the business might become an albatross around my neck. Remember, I had gone into this as a way of making my working life more flexible, to create a better quality of life for myself and my family. But one thing I learned on that course also was that, by having a better understanding of what can be done with cash flow, one can hope to stay in control. Another new concept I tackled was to ask certain clients if they would pay upfront for our services, which of course helps in our paying salaries. I did not want to go into factoring as then I might never become free and in profit. To my surprise, many clients were happy to do so. It comes down simply to finding the courage to ask.'

Is Penny good at talking about money with clients?

'No, hopeless. I hate having to do so, just as many small business people do. Usually we find here that we enjoy our work so much, we might slip into the position of giving away too much "free" time to certain clients, which in effect is being done at the expense of other clients. We have truly grown up now. The point comes where you have to look the client in the eye and explain that their needs have outrun the initial brief, and that for the work to continue they will have to pay more. Clients these days do seem to understand about quality of service and the fact that they, too, have to pay the right price.

But, again, it all comes back to that question of self-confidence; in not making the mistake of trying to be the *cheapest* in town (another common mistake of small businesses); in believing that what you are offering your clients is cost-effective solutions rather than your own cheapness.'

Attracting, and paying, good quality staff
Is there not a credibility gap in recruiting good experienced staff to a small, unproven, start-up company?

'Not really. As with the clients who have grown dissatisfied with major corporate companies, I have gained several employees who were fall-outs from the bigger agencies. These are people who have had enough of office politics and hierarchical behaviour. But, also, I have taken a lot of trouble to find the right level of people. To that end, we hired the services of a head-hunting agency to make sure we were paying for quality. Now we are working towards matching what the PR industry in general would pay. That was yet another mistake I made early on: feeling that, as we were small, we should be able to be *cheaper*. While at Cranfield, I was helped on working out the break-even points: how to organize time charts; and the fact that if we are in business we should be able to pay competitive salaries.

'Right now, our staff are all women, and I am pleased to employ women with children who prefer to work part-time, for the time being, either three days a week or for shorter hours. As I see it, I am attracting these highly qualified women from other bigger agencies, which is their loss and my gain. But we do intend to take on some men soon, just to keep the balance.'

What is different about Phipps PR from other agencies?
'One major difference is that because we have only senior executives working here, we all have our own accounts to handle. My staff tend to have different specialities, because of their varied backgrounds, but most will generalize too. As far as the client is concerned, this means they meet the account director and continue to work with her right through the project. The client gets a much better service because in effect they have a senior account director on the job full-time.

'To my mind, though, the most important consequent feature is that nothing gets overlooked. With accountability passing down the line someone tends, for example, to forget to book the photographer. Also it means we don't waste time with masses of meetings and then more meetings. From my own experience of working in bigger companies, it was awful being in the position of the junior; you were the one who took the rap for mistakes, which might have come from a poor briefing from your seniors.

'Then, too, we can be flexible about office systems if we discover they are not working. Without secretarial back-up, we have one office diary to make sure that someone is always here to answer the phones and deal with queries. We share the responsibility for keeping up to date on magazines and newspapers; outgoing letters are circulated and incoming letters are also shared, so we feed and cross-fertilize ideas. Our different client projects can sometimes be of help to each other. Every week, we meet for a brainstorming meeting and discuss what new business is coming in. Basically, though, I would say what tends to work is that we all like each other and offer each other enormous support.'

What about growth, what is the next stage?

'I don't want the business to get too big. I see it as important that we remain small and flexible, to be the sort of agency our clients want to hire. If we became too big, I would just turn into a total administrator. As it is, I tend not to go out to see clients as much as I would like. There is so much to be done with financial control, with long-term strategic planning, or worrying about whether we should network our computers; the daily running of the business and the forward planning.

'Clients need us to think strategically for their campaigns, which is where my input comes. Someone has to be able to think objectively, to stand back from the busy daily duties and offer objective and creative advice.'

Are her expensive offices really necessary?

'There is no way round the fact that image *is* important. Clients do judge you on how you look, and how you present yourselves as professionals and as a company. One of the major problems, indeed, in starting up a service industry is in selling yourself to a major company. The boss might be more impressed and willing to part with his money for a name that has instant recognizability. Bosses writing cheques need to feel reassured. So, yes, there is a performance level, whereby you are putting on a show. You need good central offices that look smart and help reflect your efficient performance. PR has had something of a bad name because it can be seen as peripheral, a waste of money spent on the freeloading press! So we also devote time to educating our clients. Our message is that in recessionary times, money invested in PR might be better spent than on advertising.

37

'But there is another hidden advantage to our prestigious offices. We lend them out to clients for their own functions; this is particularly valuable to out-of-town companies who might need to host a meeting or exhibition. The rooms are pleasant, and access is easy which is vital. We can hold press launches here and, to some jaded people of the media, maybe a different address they haven't been to before will be sufficient an inducement. Recently, for example, we hosted a Wine Society tasting here, which was a great success.'

Going back to the concept of money, and salaries, did Penny pay herself from the very start of creating this business? Or was she in some ways sheltered as a married woman and able to let the company find its feet first? At this Penny Phipps laughed and drew on an anecdote from her days at Cranfield.

'Of course, we paid ourselves! Why have a business if you cannot pay yourselves a decent salary? You might as well go to work for someone else. While I was on the course at Cranfield, they kept drumming home to us this point: as a small business, if you cannot make a 15 per cent profit per year, then for goodness sake, put your money in the building society! You'd be better off without all the hassles.'

Facts:
Staff: 6 consultants.
Turnover: £350,000.

Chapter Two

DEVELOPING A
FAMILIAR BACKGROUND

PENNY PHIPPS HAS described being compelled to find an alternative form of employment once she became a mother. Turning her own concept of PR into a fully-fledged business came at a relatively late stage, compared to other women's experiences.

So what does make others give up well-paying, potentially high-flying careers, with outside companies or large corporations, for the risky game of attempting to run their own businesses?

The impetus lies very often within their very success in traditional employment. Many women, who have turned managing director of a large corporation, have felt driven by a compulsion that they could do it all so much better by themselves. Maybe they feel that ultimately they could earn a lot more money if they were in control of the purse strings. Maybe they know that the glass ceiling hovers, either holding them down or offering far too many difficult choices: would they want a position on the company's board, even were they able to break through the mythical ceiling?

The four women, profiled in this section, are fine examples of women who firstly achieved success as employees then turned that former success to a continuing but different story as employers. The issues they have had to confront are complex in a variety of ways: for example, being a success within someone else's framework does not necessarily mean you have the wherewithal, strength or self-confidence necessary to run your own flourishing business.

Tony Blackmur

AIRDRE TAYLOR and ANNITA BENNETT
Taylor:Bennett Ltd: specialist placement consultancy for advertising and the PR industry

IN THE HIGH-FINANCE world of corporate executive placement (more commonly known as head-hunters), where clients serviced must be within the most male-dominated of corporate cultures, one might be apprehensive for two very bright and well-motivated women who decided to leave their separate careers, midway up the ladder, to venture into their own new-born agency.

Airdre Taylor and Annita Bennett have turned their fledgling head-hunting consultancy, targeted to a niche market in the advertising and PR world, from a start-up based only on a firm belief in their potential, into a thriving business that has achieved not only status but respect from clients and competitors.

The two women originally met while working with Lintas, the international advertising giant. Airdre, an Australian who graduated from Melbourne University, initially worked for RTZ in public affairs; secure and high-powered, then aged thirty-eight, she was international communications manager. Annita, a graduate from Lancaster then thirty-one, had become personnel manager with Lintas after a spell in public affairs at Unilever.

In the early eighties, these two women were prime movers in the on-going struggle for women within the corporate world. It is therefore all too easy to speculate on their decision to leave and set up their own company. Was it the infamous glass ceiling that affected their rise up the career ladder? Was it the hierarchical structure of the male office world? Or perhaps they, too, desired a better way of fitting in family life or new babies with their careers? The questions are easy to ask: but the answers are not necessarily so simple.

Taylor:Bennett has become very successful and both women are certainly now back in the high-earning brackets they previously enjoyed. Striking in their dress sense, sincere and enthusiastic in their conversation, both women are devoted to their business. They exude charm and humour. It could indeed be said that they are great communicators; unquestionably a vital attribute in their line of work. One big question is left unanswered by the women themselves and will remain open to discussion. Did they make the right decision to step out of corporate life to form their own company? Or have they, in so doing, implicitly let down other women in senior executive positions?

Why the move away from corporate life?

Airdre: 'For me, it was really the sheer frustration of being asked advice, giving it, and then watching totally different decisions being made, which I would often think were not right. Maybe the answer is that I was not one of the real professionals in that business. I really wielded no power. The response to my suggestions used to be, "Yes, very interesting, but . . . " I genuinely felt that with someone else it was time to try out our own ideas.

'Through work we became friends, but we must emphasize that the friendship was not our main starting-point. We have frequently heard stories of people who set up in business with a friend, and when the friendship collapsed the business vanished as well. But we were both business-minded people, and it was out of our professionalism that the idea grew. We both enjoyed our careers tremendously and had great fun. It was much more a question of, "Why not go and do something for ourselves?"

'The decision to leave and set up in business together was made over a couple of years. But at first we did not know what kind of business it would be. We had one aim which was to focus on something we were familiar with. We knew a lot about advertising and PR. We decided on recruitment as it represented the one gap in the market, where we could actually see that our services would be needed.'

Annita: 'While working at Lintas in Personnel, I would receive c.v.s through from head-hunters. They would be a one-page production, giving the person's name, age and a brief description which encompassed their physical and educational attributes and something about

42

their experience levels. Subsequently, I discovered that the head-hunter in question had never even *met* the candidate. They rang the person, talked through their experience and asked them what they looked like. And then they would record the information verbatim: short, dark, wears glasses! Personnel managers were dependent on this shoddy work.'

Airdre: 'It's still going on. The term head-hunter is far too widely used. What we decided to do was provide a *real* service. We bring a certain amount of psychology to our work, whereby we interview both client and candidate at length and then produce detailed reports that analyse candidates' skills, experience, strengths and weaknesses. Also we identify where those skills would relate to the job specification. Ours is certainly not a random approach, although we recognize that interviewing is not an exact science for selection.

'We knew when we were starting up that we would be offering something quite different, recognizing that there was a niche out there, for head-hunters who would research, interview, examine backgrounds in detail, explore ability and who basically *care*. We produce a report with a real assessment of the candidate's strategic abilities and skills, plus, an analysis of personality and character, as we see it, stating whether the person is likely to be a self-starter, a backroom academic, or a more streetwise type. We do not go in for psychometric testing, though our clients may follow up with that.

'The same holds true for the client, as our business is basically client-driven. We spend a lot of time learning about their business, understanding how the company operates, what are their business plans, philosophies and *modus operandi*. The client grows to trust us, and the candidates we put forward. It has happened that they will even hire somebody in advance of their actual needs, and invest in them, on our recommendations. Who knows, maybe it is very female, but we find it easy to get to know both clients and candidates in depth.'

Annita: 'It is a totally vicarious pleasure. We get to know what's going on in the industry, which major corporate companies are investing in new PR directors. We know their business plans for the next five years. Yet we also work with the smallest PR agencies, finding them staff that fit their unique philosophies too.'

But how do you leave a job one day, and set up as head-hunter the next?

'One of the keys to our success has been that we have never been pressurized by money. We both came from well-paying positions, so we were not going to starve. Also, it has to be said, we are both married to professional men with good salaries, so the actual housekeeping was not a problem. Our chairman, at the time, was a good friend and he volunteered to authorize a company loan of £5,000, which was interest free, to get us started. That meant we could rent office space – at the time we moved into cheap and cheerful rooms in Holborn. Five thousand may not seem like a huge sum today, but in 1982 it was in itself quite sizeable. The money was lent in advance against work that we would do for the company. In fact, we instantly began earning money. We have never suffered that feeling of jumping into a huge, yawning chasm . . . of debt!

'And we made it! We had given ourselves a year to plan it all out, and thought very carefully about how to position ourselves. We decided, quite simply, to be the best; never to dilute our effort. We would be entirely head-hunter oriented and provide a service that we knew was just not available. Therefore, that meant we could not advertise ourselves.

'At first, we did run a few floating ads in *Campaign*. But we were very aware of the equation between those head-hunters who advertise (the quick c.v. merchants), and those who do not (who actually think about matching real people to real jobs). From our experience on the inside, we also knew that there is a tendency to use head-hunters; people tend to respond to advertisements when they are desperate. So, apart from some initial personal contacts, all our work has come through cold calling and recommendations.

'In fact, the early Eighties being such a heyday, particularly in advertising and PR, the business quickly grew and we repaid that loan within a year. We have continued to be very cautious with money and have only ever invested as our earnings allowed. By the end of our second year, for example, we decided we could afford to invest in a computer system. When we earned sufficient money we expanded to a data base; then to hiring researchers and then to taking on more staff. Now we have a full staff complement of six. But before such growth, our major investment was from every fibre of our bodies in building up the business! You wouldn't believe the laborious lengths we went to, working from 8 a.m. to 11 p.m. every day.'

How did they learn what was needed to make such a new agency work?

Airdre: 'We made some mistakes at first, naturally. We went out together on all our interviews, as a formidable duo, which must not have been cost-effective, but it was very effective for us person-ally. We had to gain our self-confidence somewhere along the line. Sometimes, we heard in return that candidates found our interviews rather intimidating, with both of us in there grilling the poor person!

'We would go through their background and experience in detail. Bear in mind that in advertising and PR people are good at thinking on their feet. We would double check their references and what they claimed they had done. That's what I mean by the fact we are really "specialists" in the field. By now, we know so much about the industry, that if a young executive claims to have master-minded a project, we know whether he is being truthful or not. We really do *know* who is good in the business.'

Annita: 'From my informal connections with other personnel managers in other agencies, I had a bank of colleagues to phone and to whom I could explain that we had crossed the fence. We also had a direct line through to most company chairmen whom we had previously dealt with. Also, of course, I had all the knowledge of possible candidates. But, apart from that, there was nothing for it but to make a lot of cold calls.

'At first, we only had a part-time secretary as our support. We would interview three or four candidates a day, then laboriously handwrite our reports, and leave it all for her to type up on a manual typewriter. Then, we would go through and edit down our work, and she would have to retype the whole thing! The sheer volume of all that work, when you look back, is daunting. It's amazing how quickly office procedures have changed. That was only eight years ago.'

Airdre: 'The work was something of an albatross, but it was also most enjoyable. Of course, we had a lot of luck at the beginning, in the early Eighties when advertising was booming. Things would be very different if we were trying to set up now. I doubt we'd have withstood the blows to our self-confidence and optimism.'

Can they compete as a small operation with the major well-funded corporate firms in executive search?

'We're such specialists that we don't compete with the big corporations. Most head-hunters operate in the field of general management, and they know little about either PR or advertising. At first, though, we did limit ourselves by not even looking at very senior positions which needed to be filled. We pitched ourselves further down the line, imagining it would take a long time to be able to move into that senior executive level. In fact we progressed surprisingly quickly. In a way, we've moved on beyond junior management, probably never to return.

45

'You have to recognize that we've always been regarded very highly within the business, largely because we were slightly older than the average person you tend to find in recruitment. As head-hunters, what we had to offer was mature business experience with top companies such as Unilever, RTZ and Lintas, all traditional male strongholds, which meant our credibility was therefore equally high. We now know that we could or should attract more major corporations as clients. Originally, though, we had carved out our niche. We knew what we were doing and were instantly believed. Many recruitment people, after all, interview candidates without any knowledge of the business world themselves.

'But now we are not particularly devoted to spending our after-hours time on the business, as we did at first. There is an argument to say that if we were out every evening, entertaining on the social circuit, we might bring in yet more business. Maybe that should be our next challenge, to position ourselves more overtly through PR, so that we become more recognizable to the bigger corporations.'

Do they intend to keep the business small?
Is that an issue for them?

Airdre: 'Small is all very well, but the danger is that the work could become repetitive and boring. Eighteen months ago, we both realized that as the business was growing we needed to bring in an associate director. We have hired Barry Eaglestone, deliberately choosing a man who is now on our board, and who has given us a new impetus. We now have a professional team of researchers and are consciously growing our staff. We have done very well in recent years, during the time of an expansive market, so the challenge will now be to keep up the level of achievement as the market closes in.

'But we have noticed several strands that are significant in the way we operate: we are a business-based operation and can advise clients accordingly, from our own experience. For example, a FTSE [*Financial Times* Stock Exchange] 100 client recently asked us to help find them a new PR consultancy. We went through the basics, suggesting that they research their own company, so we could write up a report and brief them on their objectives. That was a very interesting exercise.'

Annita: 'To keep up the interest level, you continually have to re-invent the wheel, or at least change the wheel. Sometimes, we make ourselves take time out to look objectively at what is going on both outwardly and inwardly. We love to take on new challenges. I'd say we *drive* the business, we don't want to be led by the business.'

*

But what about family issues and flexibility in one's working life? Were they an important part of setting up on their own?

'In the first couple of years, we did let the business dominate our lives. But since then we've taken a more sensible view: that we will run the company the way we want to. We have both had babies in recent years. In fact, we managed to have our babies on the very same day! Believe it or not, most of our male clients completely swallowed the line that we had planned the whole thing. We sent out a letter, very tongue-in-cheek, saying that we were both having babies in December, pretending that somehow we had planned it all for the holiday period. Our women clients rang back, laughing down the phone, saying, "What went wrong with your planning then?" It was really very funny. Fortunately none of our clients reacted negatively.'

So how did a two-woman operation arrange time off for maternity leave if their babies arrived at the same time?

Aidre: 'Because it was my second baby, I bounced back immediately and returned to work very quickly, just taking two weeks off over Christmas. Then after a month, I took some leave to go back to Australia. Annita buried herself away at first and took a larger chunk of time off. In fact, it all worked out very well indeed. It was great.'
Annita: 'Come on, it was awful.'
Airdre: 'You say that because it was your first.'

But were they both working to the last minute?

'Oh, yes, right up to the last Friday. We were still seeing clients together.'

But now I asked an impolite question. They have already proffered the information that they came from financially well-established families. As married women, with children, did they really have to work so hard? Wouldn't it have been just as easy to dally with the consultancy as an amusing pastime? Fortunately, neither woman exploded violently in response, but they tackled the question at its face value.

Airdre: 'Quite simply, we enjoy the work and we enjoy working hard. Annita and I are both very competitive people, though fortunately not with each other. We were determined to do the best from the beginning and we do not deviate from that. Also, I think we just hit on each other luckily. We have been together for eight years now, and this partnership has worked like a dream. We don't have disagreements about what our objectives are, or our style, or why we are here, and

47

where we are going. It all keeps bobbing along on quite an even keel. It is extraordinary to find someone whose attitudes are just the same as one's own.'

Annita: 'We have the same sense of humour and that helps. For me, there was a slightly different sense of female drive: that if I'm going to do something, then I must do it well and not let people down. At the time of starting the business, I was married but had no children. I just could not bear the thought of being labelled a "housewife". It was terribly important for me to have an independent stature and a label that was not affected by my husband's professional title.'

Airdre: 'I would say we're both individualists, not traditionalists.'

But they are prime examples of today's highly educated women, who had started up the corporate ladder. Didn't they owe it to themselves, and to other women, to try to get to the very top?
Airdre: 'If it was today's world, maybe we would have broken through, I don't know.'
Annita: 'I don't honestly think I would have had the self-confidence even to think that I could get to the top.'

But would they have wanted to, were there a glimmer of possibility?

Annita: 'No.'
Airdre: 'I would have, yes. We were just ten years too soon.'
Annita: 'All I can say is, that at the time I was very vulnerable to the weakness of wanting to be liked, which was probably why I was in Personnel, because it is very "people driven". I could help other people through their problems. I doubt I would have been tough enough to make board level decisions *against* people.'
Airdre: 'If I'm honest I'd say the same.'
Annita: 'Because to act that way leads to a terrible isolation.'
Airdre: 'Some Harvard research shows that those who succeed are the ones who just don't care about other people's feelings.'

Is their niche market still the way to go?
Annita: 'There are times it may be very tempting to move outward, or expand, but we are cautious people. We'd only develop if we knew it was going to succeed.

'In the last two years, we have rekindled our commitment to hard work and although this year has seen a business downturn, in such a hard market we still have an excellent reputation.'

*

Airdre: 'Something that should be mentioned is that I can't imagine *enjoying* myself so much any other way in the last eight years, if I had not gone into this business. It has been liberating! Just think, no office politics. We have our ups and downs, but we have a good team working with us, and so far we've been doing very well indeed.'

Facts:
Staff: 3 shareholder executive directors; 3 employees.
Turnover: Profitable in 7 out of 8 years of trading.

Jacque Gill

NUALA FORSEY
Fastrack Computer Supplies

SOME PEOPLE ARE just born to succeed in business. Maybe they start out socially well-placed, from a monied background; or that it comes naturally to earn, accumulate or even to marry into, wealth. Maybe they are naturally bright, self-confident or even aggressive people who move easily through schools and universities, landing up either in top jobs or running their own show. Or, this same type may come from the very opposite background. And still they will appear to outsiders to have been 'born to succeed'.

Nuala Forsey, in her early thirties, came from Northern Ireland to live in England when she was sixteen. Because of the troubles, her family decided very suddenly to pack up and leave the war zone; that was the end of Nuala's schooling. They settled near Northampton and Nuala began to work in London – with no school examinations to boost her career. But Nuala is extremely bright, motivated, very determined and almost pathologically optimistic. Quickly, she entered the high-flying, high-earning world of tele-sales both in Canada and in England. Her success was obvious, until she decided it was time to give herself the chance of running her own company.

Personal problems, tragedies, accidents, all have dogged Nuala's life. Yet still she surfaces with a huge smile and strong conviction in her abilities and strengths. Fastrack Computer Supplies has recently taken up sizeable office space in a new business park close to Huntingdon. Very soon, she will be clocking up her first yearly million pound turnover.

To prove that she can take it all in her stride, Nuala has just treated herself to a Lotus Esprit Turbo *and* to personalized number plates. Yet she never loses sight of the significance of family, friends, and a good close relationship with her colleagues. The word indomitable was possibly invented for this woman who, unlike most men in a similar position as owner and managing director of a successful growing company, is painfully honest about her personal life.

The background that led to Fastrack

'I went into my first tele-sales job in London aged sixteen thinking "this is neat", a good job and money too. There I was, a very young, naïve Catholic virgin and of course I fell in love with someone who was older. By seventeen, I was married and the following year I had a baby. We moved up to be near my parents' home because, as one of six sisters from a very close family, that meant I always had someone to help me look after the baby. But shortly afterwards, the marriage broke up and I was on my own. I took a business course at the technical college and from there went to work for a local firm as the boss's PA. He was a smashing chap but very lazy, which was good for me as it meant that I took on more and more responsibility. I began to see that I had enough experience to move on from shorthand/typing. 'The need for money has always driven me. There I was, paying off a mortgage, having to get the baby up and out of the house by 6.30 a.m. I worked three nights a week to bring in enough cash. By 1980, I was living with another chap and we applied to move to Toronto. Surprisingly, we were both accepted and so off we went. Immediately, I landed a job there in tele-sales. I soon realized that England doesn't know where it's coming from as far as sales are concerned. That was a real boiler-house, but it toughened me up and showed me that I am a very goal-oriented person. They would set targets with incentives, and I ended up with about five colour televisions! Our job was to sell speciality advertising goods, like baseball caps, calendars and pens with advertising slogans printed on them.'

'We were paid every two weeks and got to draw on the general commission too. There I was, one of only two women and doing really well. It was shift work: 7.30a.m. – 1.30p.m. with forty-five minute sessions on the phone and fifteen-minutes break. The boss could listen into my calls at any time without my knowing. We would sit there on the phone. It was pressurized work, but on Fridays I remember getting an extra $300 counted out into my hand in cash!

'By the time I left Toronto, I was making big money. But I'd had a second child and was becoming homesick. Childcare in Canada is very good, yet one of my sisters came out to live with us and help out with the children. So I came back with everyone saying I'd never get a job here. But within two weeks I landed a great position. I had been told about the new growing computer-sales market and that you could move in there without any previous knowledge. So I went along to Pegasus Software and told them I was damn good. In Toronto, I'd learned to blow my own horn. You'd be made to stand up among your colleagues, give your own targets and say, "I'm a star!" Here they were shocked by what they called an "aggressive, pushy woman", though I'm not like that at all.

'But I was called in the next morning and was immediately offered a job. By then, I was twenty-seven. Six years ago, the computer industry was very much male-dominated. I was the first woman they had had in sales, and I was brought in as dealer-manager. But I never found that a disadvantage. In fact, I got on brilliantly for the first six months.

'Then, during one of my many long trips on the road – I was covering one third of the country and Northern Ireland – my car hit a 32-tonne truck head-on. It was a major accident, leaving me with serious head injuries, smashed ribs and a permanently damaged ankle. Even seven years later, my ankle is still a problem. I was off work for nearly a year, but after that I got back into a car and picked up my job. Even though I had young children, and my partner has always had good jobs, I knew I just had to keep on working. I'm not the type who could sit at home. I'd become a depressive. But, by this time, a new sales director had moved in and he was a male chauvinist. I'm sure he saw me as handicapped or disabled.

'I was head-hunted by a competitor and moved over as sales director. Again that was a good period as I grew a whole team; the working spirit was fantastic. At the end I was earning £25,000 a year basic, with bonus and commission, and I was driving a Porsche.

'But I was having a lot of trouble with my ankle. I'd go out on calls and would need to take a colleague with me who could drop me at the door of my appointment and then she'd go and park the car. There were times I just could not physically walk up a hill. And once a colleague playfully knocked into me at work. I fell over and was back in plaster. At this same time, while I was having to admit to myself that my leg just could not take the pace, I also discovered I had cervical cancer and had to have a cone biopsy.'

When your personal life can make a full-time job impossible
'Things were tense at home, too, because I was close to cracking up. My fatigue, and the stress involved, meant I was having virtually no

social life. Things had become strained between John and myself. I had been travelling for four years since the accident. But I'd get home at 8 p.m., by which time my ankle was so swollen that I'd have to lie down. I even remember giving dinner parties, hopping on one leg between the rooms. My ankle just could not take the daily grind.

'My doctor told me I should have serious thoughts about my lifestyle. I remember that was the worst time since the accident. I cried and cried. There was I, feeling I'd done so well. I had struggled through everything and now had to face up to the fact it was all coming to an end. Maybe it was just a dream for me to be so successful at work, earning so much, driving a Porsche!

'I took him at his word and started to alter my lifestyle, slowly. But then the real crunch came. My eldest sister, Geraldine, phoned me one day at work. She had previously had a lung removed because of cancer, and had just been told that the cancer had spread. Far worse, she now knew there was very little time left for her to live. That was the climax to my own problems too. Work and money may be important, but if you lose your sanity, what does it matter? You have to have time for family and a social life. I gave up my job. Instead, I did a little freelance work for a time. But really I concentrated on being around for Geraldine, visiting her in hospital and campaigning to find her a lung transplant.

'There was an advertisement locally for a sales manager with a small company near where we lived. Although it was not at my level, I went in to see them and was able to negotiate as much time off to visit my sister as I needed. In theory, it should have been a more relaxing way of mixing work and my personal life. But the place was horrible. I had often thought of opening my own business when I was young and living in Canada. But, since being back in England, I'd forgotten that side of things as I'd been working for such great companies. I'll tell you: one really good incentive to setting up on your own is to work for a terrible company! Then you just know you could do it better.'

Time to set up on one's own

'I'd been brought in by my new employer as a hatchet man, to clear out all the dead wood on their staff. But, after working with them for a while, I discovered that they were a talented team and a great bunch of people. So I took the sales team off the road and converted the business into tele-sales, again for the computer industry. Angela, who is still my right-hand woman, was there. But she could feel I was not happy. One day she said to me, "You won't stay here long, will you? When you go, so will I." Well, as I said the last thing on my mind at the time was starting up my own business. But the owner went on holiday and on his return, he fired me.

'A few minutes later, Angela phoned to say she had been fired too. The whole team was laid off. They ended up round at my house when Angela begged me to start my own company. There she was, just twenty-three years old and so brave; believing in me so strongly. I knew that I could not possibly take them all on, but we found them other jobs. Angela and I set up an office in the sunroom I'd just had built on to the house. Within two weeks, we had moved in two desks, a fax, phone lines and we had formed a company.

'So we started by ringing everyone we knew and immediately we were in work. This was all taking place at the beginning of August. If we had not started then, I might never have had the courage. My sister Geraldine died during a transplant operation a couple of weeks later. The family had all gone to be at her bedside for the operation. She knew she would die and said her goodbyes to us.

'It was a devastating time for me. I disappeared for ten days, unable to cope any more. But Angela battled on alone. She kept on phoning, made deals and then would rush out to buy the stock. It took us some time before we dared invest in our first £1,000 of stock. For a long time, Angela did not want us to hold any stock. She kept saying it was my money that was at risk.

'By the time I came back in to work, the business seemed to be forming itself. That in itself gave me a goal and helped me over the loss. We were having a lot of laughs, working in my sunroom during the heat of August, skipping out into the garden in our bikinis at lunchtime. But then came the next blow. I was told I'd lost the baby I was expecting. It just seemed as though everything possible was going wrong. Did it mean our business was doomed, too? It was all very depressing.

'But Angela kept saying, "I've got you into this, we *have* to make it work." And we did. Within three months, we had to move out of the house. We were working until 10 p.m., phones were ringing at all times. We rented office space across the road. It seemed far too big at the time, 300 sq foot for £400 a month. We began hiring people part-time, training up a new sales team. It was all very stressful but, the crazy thing is, once the tragedies were behind me, I realized I had never felt happier in my life or more fulfilled.'

Has expansion and growth of the business been easy?
'We moved into those offices in December 1988, and, within six months, had no space to grow any further. As we made enough money, we would hire another person. By the following December, we were really wild there; crammed in, climbing over boxes, but at the same time enjoying ourselves. My children only got to see me because the office was across the road. People kept warning me not to expand any further, but we simply had to. I moved into this space

on a business estate, just outside Huntingdon. The business park is great, being very close to all major routes of access. We'd settled in and begun to feel things were going fine.

'Then, from April to May 1990, our business took a nosedive. The crunch hit us. By the end of May, I was ready to take drastic action. The market had become very tight and everyone was cutting costs and undercutting each other. We had built up a reputation on good service, and on being competitively priced. My team is excellent and everyone is very happy working here, but we were up against other companies who did not care so much about quality. On close scrutiny, I could see that we were cutting our costs too low. Turnover is one thing, but what really matters is your profit margin. The good news is that by the next month we had re-made all our losses.

'Just before the crunch came I had applied to go on the entre-preneurs' course at Cranfield Business School. Of course I had never studied how to run a business, and certainly had no business plan when starting out. I learned so much from them. They pointed out that one should be able to plan for this dip in income. But, on the other hand, if I had had to do a business plan, I might never have set up in the first place. Had I known I would have to go in so deep financially, I probably would not have bothered. But I was so optimistic!

'One thing businesses should be encouraged to do is monthly accounts. Some will coast along for a year, thinking they are making a profit, only to find themselves severely in the red. Here, we keep daily records, our sales and income are written up on a board as we make deals over the phone, so we can all see by the hour how much we're making.

'As a business, I have made sure we are always very profit con-scious. The economy is still tight, but we have pulled up our profit margins, gone more heavily for quality of service, and this year we are on target for £1 million in turnover. I'm proud that I have some very major customers such as the Medical Research Council and Texas Homecare, nationally. But then we are bloody good at what we do. We're now in the top band of distributors.'

So what is different about Fastrack? What makes Nuala's
company tick?
On this point she is very emphatic. 'Do you know, when we were interviewed recently and one of my staff was asked the hours she works, she didn't know what they were meant to be! No-one ever takes sick days, no-one complains about staying late. I reward my team well and they enjoy helping the business grow. We're a young group. I offer them incentives, such as cars, if they perform really well. It's a fast business. We deliver 90 per cent of orders within twenty-four

hours. Everyone works to targets, Angela organizes that, and there are special rewards for achieving them.

'It's an advantage to us that, as I know from my experience in Canada, the English are so complacent about selling. My guys attempt to sell on every cold call, they won't let go easily. They also follow up every call and provide a damn good service. We pride ourselves on efficiency and on nothing going wrong. We question every mistake – unlike bigger companies. The way we work is very friendly: it's all open plan, with no private offices, no hierarchy. We help or criticize each other quite freely.

'I know I'm a good employer and that gives me a wonderful feeling of satisfaction. I have an innate sense of fairness which works well within the company. We're a real team: we cry together, cuddle each other; even the one male in our midst has become used to the openness between us. It's more like a club than a workplace.

'I can tell my team is happy when they don't begrudge working. They also never ask me for a pay rise, because I give it to them anyway, plus the cars for bonuses. I also pay higher salaries when they start to achieve better targets, with bonus and commission on top.'

Doesn't her personal life still suffer from the stress of the long hours?

'Though I have changed in the last two years, since all the personal tragedies, I'm more in control now. But my partner has always had high-flying time-consuming jobs. We have a lovely house, my eldest daughter is now sixteen and the younger child is nine. I have always been a perfectionist and wanted to keep the house spotless. But I'm beginning to say, "Heh, I can't do everything". Now I can see that I have carried the lot, and all the strain of looking after the family too. I just can't let him get away with it any more, I've begun to be more tough on him, and to demand more time for myself which has inevitably altered our relationship. Basically I'm learning to become much more selfish about Me.'

Facts:
Staff: About 6 sales force and 2 administrative people.
Turnover: Estimated £1 million this year.

Gill Cunningham

ANNE RIGG
The Business Research Unit

STARTING UP YOUR own consultancy because you sincerely believe no-one else would approach the task in quite your way may be a tempting prospect at the outset. But, finding that the business suddenly takes off, that it grows beyond all measure and that somehow, without keeping tabs on the steps along the way, you are now running a small monster with its own insatiable appetite for continuous growth and expansion, you may begin to ask: "Is this what I really wanted?"

Anne Rigg followed precisely this path with her now well-established City-based company, The Business Research Unit, a corporate and marketing planning consultancy which has grown over the past nine years from just a small one-woman start-up to a staff of twenty-one.

Anne founded her business more by accident than design. It was a combination of opportunity, the need to do good research based on high quality and the excellence of service in which she believes so earnestly, and the need to promote to clients the tangible value of research.

However she now looks back with wry humour at some of the classic business mistakes she had to ride out on the way.

'Somehow I felt I had no choice but to start my own business. I was driven to it, though I cannot really put a finger on the reasons why.

59

I remember an astrologer once telling me that I need to seek the excitement of intellectual challenge. In truth I did not really set out to have a business, I just wanted to do the work I enjoyed and have more control over my life and time. The surprise element was that it grew so large.

'I started with absolutely no business background. Rather I emerged from the academic world where I studied sociology. I did not write a business plan, nor did I have a definite strategy, I just had a cash-flow forecast. This lack of business acumen has led to certain problems, but I've survived, even though I am just not the cold-calling type of sales-woman. I started on my own, following an excellent basic training and with a growing reputation within the industry. Our consultancy brings together a real understanding of our clients' business aims, objectives and capabilities, an acute ability to recognize their customers' demands and the talent to communicate the pragmatic and potentially profitable routes for our clients.

'This success is owed in part to the excellent training and challenges set by working initially for *Which?* magazine where I worked for four years. *Which?*, particularly, helped to develop my ideas. It made me see that I do have a strong campaigning spirit which enjoys the challenge of changing people's way of thinking as a result of thorough and accurate research. I learnt the power of having the right information.'

Family influenced Anne's decision to branch out on her own, in the sense that having two children caused her to find the constraints of being an employee doubly frustrating.

'I had not decided to have children, but became pregnant just two months into my first managerial post. I felt it was my duty to the market research company I was working for to do the job for which I was hired. So I returned to work very happily almost immediately. When my second daughter was born, I was again well supported by the company and returned rather quickly. This time, however, although I was also teaching marketing to post-graduates, I found the company had changed in my absence. I missed the previous Chief Executive who had decided to concentrate on politics and I missed my daughters even more.

'So when I was offered the opportunity to do my own thing in a loose arrangement with a company on my doorstep, I moved and within a year I was a freelancer with a wonderful secretary, working from my back bedroom.

'Work loads grew and the lack of intellectual challenge which arose from working alone moved me to set up a partnership. He and I started out with similar ideas and high hopes. We rented a small office in the City, halfway between our homes. At first things went too well. We expanded out of all recognition, which was both exciting and frightening. With hindsight, I can see that we were both very able to attract new business, but neither of us had natural business acumen.

'We made all the classic mistakes: expanded too fast, hired new people, moved to bigger and more expensive offices, which added up to huge rent and overheads. We were no match for the sharper businessmen sitting on the other side of the desk negotiating office leases, leasing photocopiers and phone systems. I am still lumbered with a poor photocopier and have *eight* years to run on the lease for the phones. You really live and learn in this game.

'We were the sort of bad example they study in business school! We took our eye off the ball. The move took more time and money than originally estimated. This, coupled with the over-stretching of our existing invoicing and credit-control systems, caused the most painful time I ever experienced.

'I woke up to find that out of a passion to do my own kind of consultancy I had invented a monster with a constant demand for more turnover. Businesses are organic: as a flower grows, it needs more water. But when the work drops off, even in the short term, you can't suddenly reduce your overheads or your staff.

'We found it so difficult to find good financial advice at a price we could afford. Firstly, we are considered to be relatively small fry to most of those services so get very little attention. Secondly, and more importantly, we have never felt that any adviser has taken the time to understand our business. Many can give general business advice, but few can make it relevant to us.

'What makes us different is that we are essentially a two-month business. Although we have some good long-term contracts, much of our turnover is *ad hoc*. We are in the service industry which rarely has the tangible assets accountants are used to seeing on the balance sheets of manufacturers and retailers. Our assets are our people and, as the cliché goes, they go down in the lift every night. To the bank manager, however, they are no asset, simply an overhead.

'The other hard lesson is that some staff and suppliers suitable for the smaller business need to be replaced to facilitate the growth. We had to change our accountant and bank manager and a number of staff.'

So how is Anne handling the business side of affairs?
Anne's partner left the company two years ago. She bought out his share and has since kept on the business as her sole responsibility.

'I have been holding a turnover of £1.2 million. I took stock of my strengths and weaknesses. My strengths are clearly as a consultant working directly with clients and training staff. At the same time I recognized the need to strengthen the team who manage the business side. After a couple of false starts, I now have a strong team headed by our managing director who is also a key business getter. She is supported by our internal accountant and my personal assistant/office manager. We have had to learn to be very self-sufficient because of the difficulties of locating good advice at a price we can afford. Control of the finances is a big issue for me. I may not be strong on the details, but I'm clear on my limits. The bank took my house as security for the overdraft.

'I know if I go under my daughters and I lose our home and our only income. I know exactly what I stand to lose at any time and whether I can afford to sustain that kind of loss. At the same time, I have to say that it never occurred to me that the business would not succeed. I seem to have an in-built ability to know when I am required to shift things and within that context I am good at taking risks. This evident feeling of confidence, I think, causes the bank manager to remind me often of the vulnerability of my daughters. You have to take it and say nothing, they know that.

'I have been shocked by some of the big names in business who have come and gone in the 1980s. I wouldn't be human if I didn't sometimes query whether I might be next. I'm determined it won't be me. I'll stick to what I do well and cut my cloth if needs be.

'Our plan is not for growth but increased profitability. However, I want to avoid financial advisers who see businesses purely as money-making machines. I belong to the school that believes that flotation and the public sector can create more burdens than cures. I have seen great names and good companies in our industry disappear as a result. It may seem odd but I really think it is strange that the only criterion on which my business is judged is on how much money it generates – which has nothing to do with my initial reason for going into business.

'However, I do understand that making a reasonable income is not enough to provide the solid foundation a business needs to weather all market conditions. Hence our plans to improve overall retained profits, a fact which will please my bankers and accountants. Nevertheless, I will still gauge my success on the reactions of my clients to our work. I have a large number of blue-chip clients, household names in retail, automotive, information technology, financial and industrial markets, who keep coming back. And I have kept this complex business going for almost a decade.'

Why did Anne feel that her consultancy would offer something tangibly different from her competitors?
'Our company mission in short is "to navigate our clients to a profitable future". We don't take the helm, but we assist them to navigate their

market-place, analyse their strengths, weaknesses, opportunities and threats. In some cases we are working on an overall company strategy, in others we work on new product development, promotional strategy or specific problems.

'It matters little whether the market is new to us or is one of our specialist areas, because marketing issues are common and it is integral that we gain a deep understanding of the market of our client, prior to researching their customer base. We are not into reinventing the wheel.

'We specialize in Corporate and Marketing Planning including Total Quality Management, Customer Care, Staff Attitudes, Corporate Image and Product Usage. Every new client brings a fresh challenge and each existing client brings a new issue to consider. Each project is novel and rarely boring. Only clients can make them boring by doing our job for us. Research design is the creative part of the job and if those parameters are already set, it can be less rewarding. In our case that rarely happens as our clients are often marketing directors or managing directors who buy us to add our skills to theirs.

'Our role is rather like non-executive directors with the customer portfolio. In our presentations to our clients' decision-making teams, we bring to life their customers' opinions and demands. We assess the likely costs and benefits of meeting or not meeting those demands and from that make recommendations which, if met, will be to the initial advantage of both our client and their customer. We also report on their corporate image and the effectiveness of communications both inside and outside their companies.

'I am passionate about the quality of our service. Our clients know they come first. They don't have to follow our advice (though it's a bonus when they do). I want them to feel they get just a bit more value than they initially expected.'

Has Anne had a problem with hiring the right kind of people to keep such a company afloat?

'Each client is allocated a service team which can include as many as four staff who are charged with knowing the progress of the projects at all times. Learning to hire the right people has been the key issue. There have been plenty of good people but they have not always been right for us.

'In the early days I relied entirely on interviewing, but found that I was often clutching at straws. In desperate need for more staff I found myself easily seduced into hearing what I wanted to hear. Now we test all candidates in some way and others in the company join in the interviewing process. A business of our size cannot afford to carry anyone, it is not fair on the rest of us. Neither can we hold staff who feel it's time to move on. It can seem like a lot of hard work wasted but it is a fact of life you come to accept. We can be vulnerable to losing clients if senior people leave but our client-service teams aim to reduce that vulnerability and so far we have not lost clients that way.

'Currently, I have a really good team. We have a staff of twenty-one including six senior executives. I have become chairman and brought in a managing director from a competitor. I do not believe middle-management levels are right for our business so we do not have any. All the staff believe in our mission, work to very high standards and can cope with intermittent pressure of work very well. I have certainly felt the whole atmosphere lighten and become more fun since we have become better at recruitment.'

When you move from being a one-person service industry to heading a team of twenty-one staff, how do you justify the increased level of income necessary?

'With some difficulty. Clients can see it as us becoming more expensive. I see it as offering clients a higher level of back-up than they had with just me. Now, if I go under a bus, a client has the service team to look after them.

'Costing projects is our nightmare; recovering costs for time spent is far more difficult than costing a manufacturing process. We still charge in the main as other research agencies do on a price per interview or fieldwork unit. Clients who buy on price make comparisons that way. The sophisticated buyers assess the likely quality of input, but sadly the research is very often undervalued and treated too much like a commodity.

'A company I know of recently spent £1.2 million on a promotion which flopped. Our highest fees for a complete strategic review have been £200,000 and from that, benefit can be measured in a number of different ways which include:

- management's greater understanding of whom their customers are, how they segment and what matters to them;
- management's awareness of how they stack up against their competitors;
- a strengths, weakness, opportunities and threats analysis;
- recommendations of potentially profitable directions; indeed we probably could have told the management that that particular promotion would have flopped.

*

'Research does not answer all the questions, nor should it. The role of the experienced, intuitive and decisive captain of industry is still of paramount importance.

'However, we are naturally proud of our successes and can list our recommendations which have been proved right. We have a portfolio of letters from satisfied clients, including one from a client who saved £250,000 by spending £4,000 on research. But costing our worth is still our major concern.

'Our future strategy depends on us getting a better answer. I see things very simply, a fee equates to so much for direct costs, paid to get fieldwork completed and analysed. The remainder makes a contribution to fixed overheads. When total contribution exceeds total overheads, The Business Research Unit moves into profit. These figures provide monthly turnover targets assuming we keep to roughly the same proportion of direct costs on each job.

'I like to keep things straightforward in my mind. I've been shaken in the past to see how creative accountants can be: for example, we have now moved to a pessimistic form of accountancy, with which I feel safer! I know what I need to bring in, in terms of turnover, plus, what my monthly and annual targets should be. These are the figures I keep in my head at all times.

'We have some continuous projects; we also have to go out and find new work. The key, to my mind, is in keeping overheads down. As soon as you develop a loose attitude towards spending money, you have stepped on the slippery slope to disaster. Having said that, currently we are investing in a total quality management programme for the business, which is expensive for a small company. But I believe it is of real benefit to us. Also we have to do what we are advising clients to do, manage our own change and development. In truth, running a business can be an enormous headache, and there are times when I wouldn't wish it on anyone!

'The biggest problem arises from trying to keep all your plates up in the air, at any one time. In this week, for example, I brought in two major new projects. Do I take on new staff to help us with the workload, and then worry when work falls off again? Do I say I simply cannot handle the two at the same time? Of course not. We get on and do them both. But I do wonder sometimes why I am taking on all these headaches. I could *contract* the company, I could return it to a much smaller staff size, working instead as a one-woman guru.

'Few people deliberately contract a business, yet it is probably a decision more should consider. However, I know I would not now feel content, being unable to offer the same quality of work. And for that, I do need to have my specialized team.'

*

65

The emotional side of being a woman in charge of her own business

'Although I know I need to work, my children are the most important people in the world to me. I am passionate that they have a better start in life emotionally and more opportunities than I did. I must, therefore, balance my life carefully to meet their needs. As a mother, I need to come in to work not worrying about things at home. I have developed a network which supports my lifestyle and provides my children with the best alternative care I can get. If you could see a week of my life, you might wonder how I manage. I have to travel out of town quite considerably. I am also a single parent, though the children see their father on a regular basis.

'My personal life seems to have narrowed down to two elements: my children and my work. And little else. When a marriage breaks up, if you're running your own business, you realize how vital a supportive husband or partner can be. Setting up a business in itself can drive a marriage into the ground. You are likely to be working far too hard on the business, for your husband's liking. You may be bringing in more money than he is. Every apparent lack of devotion and duty to the family will be noted.

'I'm sure I am a workaholic, but then it seems the huge number of hours I put in are necessary. I try to get home for my children's bedtime. But then, after 9.30p.m. I start working again, often till 2a.m. (or even later if needs be). That is when I write up reports and do my thinking. I prefer to work in the middle of the night. I'm one of those people who does not need much sleep. In fact, my best work tends to come when I'm most pushed. On Saturdays, my greatest pleasure is to stay in bed watching children's television with my daughters; I have also encouraged them to share my passion for the theatre. I know that I do not want to go on like this forever, but right now I have accepted that a good emotional life requires time which, sadly, I just do not have.

'It is ironic in some ways in that the money I make enables me to have a decent home, the support of a full-time nanny and someone to do the garden, all of whom I need, only because I work.

'Yet money has certainly been the least motivating factor. Some people imagine the boss makes all the money. But it is not quite like that. They see "free" cars, and "free" lunches. But there really isn't anything "free" in life, is there? Each month I draw the same salary as my most senior member of staff; any extra money goes straight back into the business. No, I'd say that I'm not greedy for money. More importantly, I enjoy my life and my work.

'As a single person, the positive side of the equation is that I do get a lot of satisfaction from the respect and support of my clients. Also, it does mean that I am able to give them that last piece of myself and my time, which otherwise might be reserved for a partner. Not having that balance for myself means that much of that unused emotion goes into the business.

'But it has to be said that being a woman, a mother and running a business, can make me seem like a Martian within the wider social context. People assume I'm formidable or frightening. They probably assume I'm mad! I guess, however, that I might have been more successful, even more quickly, had I been married to the right person: maybe to a man who was an accountant!'

Facts:
Staff: 21, including 6 senior executives.
Turnover: About £1.2 million a year.

Chapter Three

COMING IN FROM
THE COLD

SETTING UP YOUR own business from a strong base of a wealth of expertise, professional knowledge, and fund of ready-made contacts, or well-established reputation, is to encounter one set of problems. But what about those women who deliberately seize on an idea, and believe that somehow, with all possible blind faith, they will *make* it work?

As Emma Bridgewater showed in the first chapter, it is possible to take a manufacturing idea and make determined bold moves to set up a process by which a product is made, distributed and sold – successfully. The two women behind Blooming Marvellous made a very similar bold decision with their plan to launch a mail-order service selling maternity clothing. In their situation, it was very much a case of two women recognizing a gap in the market – as they had themselves been unable to find the right sort of pregnancy clothing – and following that idea through to its logical conclusion. Vivienne Pringle and Judy Lever started their business the slow, cautious way, beginning in the back room of one of their houses, while both continued working during its first few years.

The other women in this chapter, Gillian Harwood and Jan Morgan, landed up in the property business, both, as they point out, by default rather than design. They are examples of women who received that invaluable push while housewives, non-working women somewhat tied down by young children, that can come about when a marriage or partnership breaks up. Both women tell fascinating stories of stumbling across deep pockets of entrepreneurship within themselves; of locating amazing abilities to fight back, persevere against the odds and emerge at the other end with the understanding that they are good business-women, born ideas-people, and also very talented employers.

All three stories show tremendous 'chutzpah'; these are women who closed their eyes to problems ahead, their ears to people warning them not to be so foolish, and their hearts to any fears or remorse. You may require good business sense, somewhere along the line, but you will never find out whether that business sense is lying dormant behind your former self-image, unless you try.

VIVIENNE PRINGLE
and JUDY LEVER
Blooming Marvellous: maternity and baby clothes by mail order

IT MUST BE the dream of many women to create a mail-order business based on some element of fashion or style; to be in the position whereby you can sell to other like-minded souls what you yourself consider to be tasteful, or necessary, or simply goods you know would be hard to locate in the shops. Blooming Marvellous is just that: a mail-order company selling maternity clothes, as well as baby's and young children's clothing, that fit the style of today's younger generation of mothers.

But to come into this field from the outside, without being able to sew a dress or blouse themselves, and make a huge success out of the business in just nine years, has to be a remarkable feat. Vivienne Pringle, now thirty-five, came from the advertising world. She started her working life as a secretary, and worked her way up to junior account executive in a small advertising agency. Eventually, while still in her early twenties, she became director and part-owner of the agency. By the time she was twenty-five, Vivienne was a shareholder and earning a healthy salary.

Judy Lever, who has just turned forty-three, started working in television straight from university, first as a researcher, moving into production and direction of current affairs and documentaries. Hardly the most likely partnership to set up a fashion mail-order business.

Before we launch into the story of how Blooming Marvellous came into being, it is worth looking at the one reason Judy and Vivienne feel is most likely responsible for their success.

How did they take a small backroom idea, one they initially knew nothing about, into a thriving business success?

Vivienne: 'Essentially, what we are about is production and marketing. The fact we are selling maternity and baby clothes is almost irrelevant. Much more important is how we get the catalogues into people's hands; how we keep up with the orders; act efficiently; get the right price on the product; and continue to keep up our publicity so sales do not contract. When you think about it, we came from a sophisticated background, in that sense, with a lot of "inside" knowledge; not about how to make clothes, but about marketing, advertising and promotion.'

Judy: 'My research base from television meant, too, that I was not intimidated by having to find things out. I was never put off by the often daunting prospect of going out there and asking questions, when we really had not a clue how to start. Another company may have wonderful designs, but if they cannot get them made, or know how to shift the catalogue, they will never get beyond the kitchen table.'

Vivienne and Judy were long standing friends. In 1981 Judy was pregnant and could find nothing to wear that seemed appropriate.

Judy: 'I was complaining about this fact, and commented that there must be a gap in the market because, if someone like myself could not find decent maternity clothes in the heart of London, what must it be like elsewhere? All I wanted would be described as ordinary, nice clothes, the kind of normal wear I usually go around in, along the lines of straight-legged trousers and up-to-date sweatshirts. And I wanted to find such clothes at a reasonable price. Back in 1981, the only maternity clothes available were either very cheap and nasty, or very expensive.

'I know that a lot of women then were buying maternity clothes at Laura Ashley, not because their clothes were designed for maternity wear, but just because she was making big loose smocks. They were not very suitable, because if that type of dress did not suit you before you were pregnant, if like me you tended to be short and big-busted, then once you were well into pregnancy you could look like the side of a house! One thing I quickly learned, during my own pregnancy, is that whereas in the early months it might be fine to wear large sizes, or your husband's shirt and jeans, towards the end you need clothes that are cut properly, that do not accentuate the negatives.'

Both: 'We set up in 1982, in a very small way. At the time, neither of us was looking to leave our jobs. This was not meant to be a business that would take us away from those careers. At first we created two styles and a simple leaflet for distribution in some ante-natal clinics, which had a limited success. Our first breakthrough came when we placed a tiny advertisement in a specialist magazine. That brought in quite a response. Then the photographer we worked with managed to arrange for a photograph of one of our outfits to be included in an editorial spread for a magazine. That really got us started.'

Surely they were jumping several stages here. If they knew nothing about making clothes, or selling them, how did they ever arrange for those two styles to be made, promoted and distributed?

Judy: 'First we went round all the street markets looking at fabrics. Neither of us is capable of sewing, which possibly was our saving grace. Never for a moment did we intend making our designs up in our back bedrooms.'

Vivienne: 'Also, it was never our idea that it would become a little cottage industry. Had we even so much as attempted to make the clothes ourselves, we'd still be selling a few a week, not hundreds, certainly not thousands. Right from the beginning, we felt that if it was worth doing it was worth doing well. That way we could grow bigger. We knew we had to find a manufacturer. What we didn't know was how!'

Judy: 'It began with my going around to visit a list of factories and becoming more and more depressed, until finally I came across one that seemed amenable and whose quality of work was up to our standards; more importantly he was prepared to take on our very small run. At the beginning, we had a hundred of each style made up. To us that seemed a huge commitment at the time. But looking back I can see that it was very nice of the factory to take the trouble.

'We found fabric that we liked after quite a search. We had had to give up on markets, and go to the warehouses. The two original styles were the items we felt were most missing: a denim pinafore dress and another dress in a print fabric that was just pretty. As to the design, we had to find a pattern cutter. Even saying that sounds as though we knew what we were doing! But we actually did not know that the person we were looking for went under the name "pattern cutter".

'We'd drawn up the basic design ourselves, and knew where the seams should go, but we needed the person who takes that sketch and makes it into the kind of pattern you would buy were you sewing at home. We looked through *Drapers' Record*, the trade journal, and found someone who was really helpful and supportive. She had never made maternity clothes before, either. Now, of course, we have our own pattern cutters. But we still do the initial design ourselves.'

Did they have to invest a lot of their own money? Or go to banks to borrow?

Vivienne: 'We put in about £1,000 each of our own money. Then we went to the bank for an overdraft facility of £10,000. We had written up a business plan, but really at that stage it could only be a projection. Yet, we had had a fantastic response to that first editorial. Some two thousand people had contacted us; not all to buy the garments, of course, but at least they wanted to see our catalogue.

'Back then, we were using Judy's home address. After work, we'd go to her house and pack catalogues on one day, and orders on the next. Very soon, we found we had to employ an independent mail-order house. And, quite soon after that, we established our own warehouse. The catalogue grew from being a simple leaflet, as we added more styles. Quite quickly we went into full colour and concentrated more heavily on the quality of the production. From my work in advertising, I knew about printing and putting together professional-looking brochures or promotional material.'

Was costing the products a problem at the beginning?
Judy: 'At first, it was very difficult. I suppose we learned through trial and error. I'm glad that we began so small, as we were able to creep along through the learning curve! Now, we have a formula for pricing. By systematically researching as we went along, we tried to protect ourselves against being ripped off. When you're very green, and you go into an area about which you know nothing, particularly perhaps if you are women, that is a danger. We did talk to some other women in a similar kind of mail-order business in the early days, and they gave us an idea of some of the pitfalls ahead. But, in the end, we probably have to say that we've been very lucky. The factory did not rip us off, they continued to produce quality goods. But, knowing as little as we did, we could have fallen flat on our faces.

'At the beginning, we both still had our careers, so the business was kept quietly simmering on the back burner. Within a year or so, we had employed quite a few people, although we still could not afford to give up our full-time jobs. When I eventually did stop working in television, to concentrate on Blooming Marvellous full-time, I had to take a big drop in salary. There was no way we could have afforded such huge payments then.'

When did they decide Blooming Marvellous was strong enough to carry them both full-time?

Vivienne: 'I gave up first, when I was pregnant with my second child. We both had babies and had returned to our full-time jobs quite quickly. We were both very happy with those careers. But, of course, that kind of work is very demanding and, once you have children, those demands can seem too high. I realized I'd rather spend my time doing what I wanted to do, creating something of our own. Judy gave up her job six months later.

'We decided that we'd try going full-time with the business, for a year or so. Then, if it did not work out, we could have gone back into our former careers without loss of face. Any working mother might try something similar, without losing out too badly if she has to return, particularly if she has already established a reputation and a senior position.

'At first, we both agreed to take relatively low salaries which would help carry the business through. When we had concentrated on it part-time, we didn't pay ourselves at all. But then we had ploughed all the money back into making the business work.'

So how did they make the business grow once they had both joined full-time?

Vivienne: 'The business had already grown quite large. We had the warehouse where we employed four women to do the mailings for us. They have been wonderful all through the years, taking a lot of responsibility on our behalf. We were able to trust them, which has been a real boon. In a sense, they handle all the mail-order administration, leaving us to concentrate on design, PR and marketing. Of course, we have had to face up to problems, such as stock not coming in on time and angry customers. With maternity clothes, there really is not any time to lose.

'At first, we were doing everything ourselves from Judy's house. Then, just over three years ago, we took on an office in Central London. Now we have a lot of space, and yet we are about to move in to even greater space. There are seven of us working at the London base: a financial controller, PA, pattern cutter, designer, production manager, and ourselves; and twenty-five staff at the warehouse.'

*

Judy: 'Before we both became full-time, we never had a minute to concentrate on how we could grow the business. So, once we had decided to develop it, that is what we did. We devoted time and energy to thinking about how to make the business better, and more cost-effective. At times, it is rather like painting the Severn Bridge, that you have constantly to reassess every aspect, to say what needs improving. How can we be more efficient? We try to keep up the exercise all the time. You cross a Rubicon at some point with mail-order sales, when you become big enough to have gathered a name. Magazines usually approach us now about features. But there are always new pregnant women to be reached. It is never a passive market. And time is always of the essence. Pregnancy is a very limited time.

'Although our overdraft facility has been increased over the years, we do not borrow heavily. There are certain levels of debt we won't go beyond. One of the dangers when you begin is that you can be so dogged down in the every-day minutiae that you feel constantly busy. But you may be spending your time on the wrong things, worrying, for example, whether the shipment of buttons reached the factory on time.

'What Vivienne and myself should be worrying about is what *type* of buttons and what styles we should be promoting; or what other methods we could employ to carry the business forward. Someone else should worry about the nitty-gritty details. That is an important lesson to learn.'

What do they perceive to be the greatest problems of small businesses?

Vivienne: 'You may not have enough money to employ other people, so you let yourselves become bogged down. Yet, it can only be after you delegate work to someone else, that you can let yourself grow. Relatively recently we have taken on more staff. What happened was, because we acquired the warehouse quite early on, it felt as though we had taken on the staff we needed. We imagined that we were capable of doing everything else.

'In truth, we were rushing around between factories, worrying whether they were all producing on time. We might have ended up spending four days of the week out of the office, sorting out such problems. Eventually, we sat down and talked it through. Then we realized we should devolve those responsibilities on to someone else, who would be *better* at that kind of detail than ourselves.

'We analysed the core needs of *our* time; isolating those aspects of Blooming Marvellous which it was absolutely crucial we remained in control of, and what work could be devolved. Rather obviously

78

perhaps, managing the factories and the bookkeeping were areas to farm out. Unbelievably, until then I had done all the bookkeeping – though I hated doing it!'

How did they go about finding a production manager, again an area of which they knew nothing?

Vivienne: 'We looked in the trade press and discovered an agency that hired such people. We interviewed and took on the man we liked best. That has been such a great leap forward for us. He makes the production run a lot more smoothly than we ever could. Now he needs an assistant, so we will be hiring someone else soon. Very often, I find that, by the time you come to recognize such a need, the need is already a necessity. This is an inherent problem for a small business, because you might be destroying the company in the meantime.

'We now have twenty factories making our garments. And we send out many thousands of catalogues a year. The catalogue is our one major expense, but then it is our basic point of sale, because we are totally mail-order. We have had a look at going into retail, but so far have decided against that route. There are plans afoot, however, to widen the business further. But I won't divulge any more information than that. We're always coming up with new business ideas!'

Why did the business grow so big, so quickly?

Vivienne: 'We were probably helped by the fact neither of us could sew. The PR and marketing expertise are most important. Also, the fact we almost immediately produced a full-colour catalogue. And that we found a factory manager who initially would work with us on short runs. We stuck to our business beliefs and refused, for instance, to alter the pattern for individuals. That is another aspect of not letting yourself be trapped by the cottage industry mentality.

'I think we have discovered that we both have business minds. When we had our children, for example, we did not sink into motherhood. We had already returned to our jobs and were committed to working, as well as hopefully being halfway adequate mothers! We have always seen the business as a "proper job", with long hours and ultimate commitment. Obviously, we can also continue working when we are at home. I might plan out an advertising strategy or write copy when I'm back with the children in the evenings. It is really a question of commitment.'

Judy: 'We have had some ghastly financial problems, but have never been too scared, or lost too much sleep. We've managed to remain optimistic and determined. Many people are now dependent on us for

79

their livelihoods, which of course is a responsibility in itself, but also a great challenge.

Are there any regrets for giving up what were significant and interesting former careers?

Judy: 'Business is much more creative than I'd imagined. When I was at university, I'd have frowned at the very word. In reality, I find we use our creative skills as much now as we did in our previous jobs, which appeared more glamorous. The very building of a business is creative and also great fun. There are ups and downs to employing people. But when they are loyal, and you enjoy working with them and they obviously enjoy working for you, and really want to stay on, then that is a great plus.'

And what about their partnership, what is the secret of its success?

Judy: 'We share the major parts of the business, the designing of the clothes, decisions, choices over who we employ and where we are going. But basically I think we are lucky that we get on incredibly well, especially when you look back at the early days. We have the same sense of humour which helps. But, maybe more important, we have the same sense of commitment. And we trust each other over time issues. I never have to think, "Huh, Vivienne's not working hard enough!"

'We also share taste. We seem to choose the same fabric every time. If we looked at swatches of a thousand fabrics we'd both come up with the same one.'

What about juggling children and working hours? Have these two women found a solution to being able to blend a career and family life?

Judy: 'We take time off for school sports days and the like. If a child is ill and needs us of course we'd stay at home. But we take our time openly and honestly, not exactly computing our hours, but it just seems to work evenly.'

Vivienne: 'Maybe I take more time, because I have three children, and Judy only has two. But I would say I am working harder now than in my advertising days. There, I might have worked longer hours, but here more is achieved. When I was in advertising, if I had to work on a Sunday I would have resented the time. But now I find it fun. If I come into the office over a weekend, I'll bring the children with me.'

*

What about the future? What are their plans?

Judy: 'We won't sell out. We have lots of plans and certainly won't be standing still. But, apart from that, no clues. The competition is rife in this business!'

Facts:
Staff: 7 in London, 25 at the warehouse.
Turnover: They will not divulge any figures.

GILLIAN HARWOOD
United Workspace:
managed business centres

THERE ARE ALWAYS certain women who appear to have been dragged into running their own business; not necessarily kicking and screaming, but who suddenly find themselves alone on the raging seas, mastering the helm.

At this juncture, it seems appropriate to pay tribute to many women's great initiative, enormous skill and intuitive powers, in business life. Far from any recent stereotype of women, showing them as incapable of making sound financial decisions or business judgements, so many seem to adapt all too easily to the necessities and complexities of running their own show.

Where Gillian Harwood is concerned, the particular driving force could be defined as the discovery, one day, that the man in whom she had entrusted not only much of her emotional life, but also a large proportion of her financial stability, was an insecure, untrustworthy human being. Nearly bereft, with two young children, Gillian took the necessary steps to protect them from penury. Over the years, this charming woman, who has moved into an enviable position, managed to carve out for herself an innovative business built solely on her own drive and determination.

Workspace, one of many business offshoots that now make up the property interests of Gillian and her current partner, derived from her concept that dilapidated buildings could be renovated and transformed into small units for new businesses. They could be rented on a monthly no-strings-attached basis. Finding the capital investment for such a brilliant, but capital intensive idea, was Gillian's real coup.

Gillian describes herself, when younger, as the type of girl who had no idea what she wanted to do. She was persuaded by her father to take up secretarial training. However, before leaving school she had taken some vocational guidance tests, where it was pointed out that she would make a good architect. It seems ironic that after all the contortions of her life, she finally has found herself involved with the imaginative recreation of properties. Gillian has never received any formal training, but has always loved buildings; a passion that has seen her through some very hard times.

Her early chequered career took her from secretarial college, to travelling around America, then to a job with the BBC Drama department as a secretary ('hair-raisingly awful!'). She tried teaching for a few months but hated that.

'I never really found my feet about any form of career, so in a sense I just dropped out. I started a small business with an antique stall in Kensington Market, and learned a bit about wheeling and dealing. Then, because I'd always been vaguely creative, I started my own gardening business which was very popular. Now it would be mega-business but then, in the early Seventies, there was no competition and my phone never stopped ringing. I could have built that business up, but began having children, and I just naturally gave it up.

'My grandmother had left me £4,000, out of which I put £2,000 into a cottage in the country (in 1968), and the remainder I used as a down-payment on a big old Victorian house in Wandsworth. It had been turned into bedsitters and was a real dump. But I was living then with the father of my children, whom I never married though we were together for fourteen years. He was pretty much a ne'er do well and hopeless at looking after money, so I began taking in foreign students for bed and breakfast.

'That kept the wolf from the door and made growing up much more fun for the children. I was a late Sixties' type of mother, keeping hens in the garden and baking bread. It's extraordinary to look back because now I can barely open a tin of baked beans! But the man I was living with invested in property in Camden Town. He'd bought the tail end of a defunct business, and a company name from a relative of mine, intending to build up a business there. To help him out I had guaranteed a bank loan to the extent of £6,000.

'But, of course, everything went wrong. One day I was at home, with a toddler and a baby, when a registered letter arrived saying the bank was foreclosing on the loan that I had guaranteed. I had seven days in which to come up with £6,000. This was 1974, and I can tell you that six thousand was an awful lot of money! It represented about half the value of my house. But I knew I was not going to lose my house over him.

'It was then, I suppose, that I realized I had a fighting spirit. I informed the bank who were holding the mortgage that the property itself was an asset and, that as I had experience of doing up properties, why would they not lend me a *further* loan, on which I would renovate the building into small business units. The idea had come to me from personal experience: 1) in letting out bed sitters and 2) at the antique market, when we small-time entrepreneurs had been allowed to rent our space for as long as we needed or could afford, all sharing one larger commercial area.

'Needless to say, the bank told me I was being ridiculous, that I had no experience of business, and that they had never heard of renting out one hundred square foot units. The concept has now become known as "workspace" and is very popular, especially since the last decade's growth in small start-up businesses.

'I then wrote my first letter to a bank! I addressed myself to the Chairman, saying I felt it was strange to have been turned down so flatly, when I had come up with a good idea, during a six-week stay of execution wherein I was supposed to think of a viable proposal. At the same time, I read a newspaper article about an architect who had converted a similar building elsewhere in London. I phoned him and asked his help with my building in Camden. He agreed to come and look it over; at the same time I asked his secretary which bank he was using for a loan. I went to see that bank manager, and they agreed to take over the loan.'

How has Gillian managed to bring off such remarkable tricks so often?

'I'm not sure, but it must be that I have a very forthright manner. I needed to raise £35,000 to convert the building. My mother offered to put in £10,000, and the bank would lend me £25,000. The real catch-22 of raising capital, I discovered, is to be able to do so without putting your own home on the line. Fortunately, that tiny little cottage I had bought a few years previously became my one asset.

'Everything that could possibly go wrong went wrong. Work progressed on the Camden building, but the builders went bust. In the end, I had to finish off the painting myself, with two young children hanging on to my skirts. Then I had to start the letting process from home; when the phone rang there would always be a baby crying in the background. I was forever rushing from Camden to Clapham, because I could not afford real childcare. I'd rely on a muddle of arrangements, or maybe you'd call it a network of help, including my mother. This was not part of the Yuppie ideal, with a super nanny there to help me out. It was all done the poor way!'

Bitten by the property bug, Gillian was successful in letting out that first building. Small businesses were growing. Most people could not find anywhere cheap or easy to rent without becoming entrenched in a lease. And, because of the planning laws, London was full of derelict warehouses and factories.

'I saw another building with a "To Let" sign outside – in the heart of the West End – and I became very excited by its prospects. I wondered if I could do the same thing again. The site seemed ideal and the building, I could tell, would be attractive if rescued by loving hands. But how would I raise capital a second time? I returned to the bank manager, who offered to support me if I could come up with one third of the cash. I tried all means: I advertised for capital investors, I tried to find tenants who would come in with a payment upfront. Then, out of the blue, I was introduced to a group of Islington architects who were looking for a cheap space to rent in the West End.

'Eleven years ago, I met the architects who helped make Flitcroft Street become a reality. This was where my partnership with Philip Lancashire began. The architects agreed to come up with the equity share, in return for space for themselves, and the bank would lend me the £75,000. But then it all went wrong again. The bank backtracked after all my efforts, because it was 1979, and we were in the midst of the real credit squeeze. The bank manager was very apologetic, but his head office had turned him down. I had been struggling to raise the one third, for six whole months, and he just shook his head and apologized. This time I wrote a letter to the chairman of Barclays.

'We dressed up my boyfriend's son as a messenger; he cycled the letter over, and was rushed up in the lift to the chairman's office. Within an hour and a half the bank manager had received a phone call from his Head Office giving me the go-ahead. How had I worked it? Who knows. But I had not been reticent. I'd outlined my achievements; emphasized how Barclays were making all the right noises about small business but, when it came to it, were doing nothing. I also said that at the end of the week we were planning to hold a press conference to announce the start of the Flitcroft Street project, which would reflect well on their bank. We got the money and the building has become a huge success.'

*

86

Yet I felt that Gillian, rather as the Blooming Marvellous women had done before, was glossing over some of the most important factors within the business process. Jumping in and borrowing large amounts of money from the bank may be one notch in the belt, but when property development is so capital intensive, with such a long lead time before you can hope to bring in any income, how did she work out to cover the repayments?

'Sometimes, I learned that the bank will give you a nine-month holiday on interest repayments; or they roll up the interest until you start bringing in income, depending on when you feel you will be making any money. At that time, the business prospects were good because, unlike now, there was a dearth of commercial space in central London. We were determined to make it into a success and, using Philip's architectural expertise and contacts, we quickly brought in designers and started up the renovation.

'Philip and I have worked together ever since. We soon moved on to the next building project, which was Omnibus, the old City of London horse-drawn omnibus factory in Islington. It was a huge site close by King's Cross and St Pancras Stations; ideal for our vision of small unit workspaces. The building was in a dire state, but we fell in love with it, and took on an eight-year lease (as it was not available to buy). Again we fell into problems with the bank over borrowing yet more capital. Again I wrote, this time a virtually identical letter to the chairman of yet *another* bank, and sent it off by messenger. This time I had to wait two days, but the message was the same. The local bank manager was given the go-ahead.

'Oh, the power of the written word! I did have a fairly good education, with several O levels, and I can write a reasonable letter. But it shows that it *really* does pay to go to the top. And never take No for an answer. Those crummy old clichés do mean something.

'We were renovating the Omnibus building throughout 1980–81. If we think business is bad now, we should remember there was massive unemployment then, around three million. Margaret Thatcher had just come in and interest rates had gone up to 20 per cent.

'Omnibus is now well established, with about eighty small firms, often as quite long-term tenants. We offer the small company low overheads, and all-inclusive monthly costs with no additional capital to raise. All the back-up facilities of a normal office are on site: there is a receptionist, complete secretarial services, conference rooms, photo-copying and a kitchen. The design is light, bright and airy – so it's a cheerful, bustling sort of place in which to work. Just recently, we extended even further by taking over the building next door.

'We had great plans for this new building. But this time we have been somewhat stymied by the recession. There aren't too many new businesses starting up and seeking premises. However, with the new round of redundancies, I'm sure we'll be seeing the next wave of the once-employed turning to their own consultancies.'

Are there other plans afoot other than the Workspace units?
'Yes. In a sense we've already moved on from there. Since Philip and I met, we have gone on to form many different companies and to diversify; indeed, it is interesting to see how one progresses. We have been full of brilliant ideas over the past decade, though things have quietened down with the recession coming on. Recently, we have worked together on a shopping centre in Lewes, Sussex, which has been a terrific success and a major tourist attraction for the area. Our biggest claim to fame, however, has been in Mortlake, West London. In 1989, we entered a competition for a development on a marshland site down by the river. We were up against the likes of McAlpine and Wates, but we brought to the area a plan to incorporate workspace units, a youth club, some flats and a lovely restaurant. The competition was run democratically for the local residents, and they chose our scheme.

'Mind you, having won the competition, everyone then told us we were mad. All our potential backers withdrew, and again we returned to the problem of raising the finance. But we raised the money, the project is complete and, in the end, we have won four design and conservation awards. As far as income goes, it will not do much for our company as we had to give away 90 per cent of the equity to raise the capital. But it does show that you have to keep on pushing. The prestige involved has been quite spectacular.

'By default, at the same time we were introduced to our next business venture which is running restaurants. The one we designed and had built in the Mortlake scheme has been so successful that it has led on to more of the same. We just seem to know instinctively how a restaurant should be run; what kind of place people *enjoy* eating in. We give good value for money and provide a great sense of style. The restaurant has a busy, bustling and inexpensive atmosphere – and it is in a pleasant environment looking out over the river.'

What are Gillian's views now on a business life?
'I've taken phenomenal risks in the past, in fact I always seem to be forced into the risk-taking position. I have mortgaged my own house over the years, four different times. My little cottage is still lodged with the bank as collateral. You have to have a bulkhead philosophy, that you will retain some security so you can sleep a little bit at night!

'But we have always kept things tight. I sub-contract out mostly. We've never had many employees. Recently, now that times are more difficult, we have cut back on staff. My own management style is to delegate *everything*, as long as I know I can trust people. We really have a tiny little company. The turnover may be £2-3 million, which for property developers is peanuts. But we literally run on a staff of five people and my dog!'

Would she have gone so far had she not met and joined in partnership with Philip?

'In a sense, the first man in my life, as he was so hopeless, was the spur that got me going. One thing I do find about being a woman in business, is that it can be very lonely. Without Philip around as my support, I might have given up before now. I remember times I would feel quite hurt, when all the "girls" in our office would go out for a drink together and would not think to ask me – because I was the *boss*.

'But I have discovered that I enjoy the business side of the work. Although I never did well in Maths at school, now I *love* doing cash flows and projections, budgeting and costing. I'm sure a lot of women are unnecessarily afraid of Maths. As Mrs Thatcher has said, it all comes down to using our basic "housewifely" skills.

'I've gone an awful long way on common sense and integrity. But, it has to be said, that being your own boss is miles easier than trying to work for a corporate bank in the City. Having to answer to other people all round, that would be hard. On your own, you can work on a hunch that you'll make it, without having to answer to anyone else. I would always recommend to other women that they become their own bosses. We're so good at making our own decisions.

'As for the risks, as I see it, when your back is against the wall you'll go out there and do anything. One factor that has always saved me is that I really don't care too much about money. Worse things can happen to me than that I lose it all. I'd just give up and live off the State. I'm not motivated by money at all. It is a question of doing something, achieving great heights, that has meaning for me. I've never been very interested in spending much money. I work far too long hours to enjoy spending it! Philip and I don't live together, but we share a farmhouse at weekends. If I entertain, it would be there; never in London. I still live in the house in Wandsworth. I suppose if things were really bleak, I could always go back to letting out rooms!'

Facts:
Staff: 5 people and a dog.
Turnover: £2 – 3 million.

JAN MORGAN
Grosvenor International:
commercial and residential
real estate

AT THE BEGINNING of the chapter, I mentioned the terrific impetus that can come to a woman's business life, or business acumen, when she is divorcing, or when possibly she finds herself on her own with children to support. The situation can arise to women of any social class. It may come as a surprise to the woman herself to discover this new 'businesslike' layer of her personality buried deep behind the 'happy housewife/mother' façade.

The association between women and property should not, however, come as a surprise, least of all when we consider how much of a woman's time and energies can be devoted to the home. Historically, maybe she engineered the buying and selling of the family's houses, even though the money would have come from her husband. Very likely, it was the woman who master-minded all interior decoration and organized any exterior repair work too. Jan Morgan is another woman who, like Gillian Harwood, suddenly found herself thrown into the world of property when her marriage was on the verge of breaking-up.

Jan had always moved in well-heeled social circles. Nevertheless, when facing the prospect of being out on her own, as she puts it, she realized she was 'totally unemployable'. A former nurse, with a smattering of art training, the mother of two young children, Jan had also had a brush with cancer in her late twenties. She says enigmatically, 'I was not going to be high on anyone's list as an employee! I also had an identity crisis: I was the wife of a charismatic and famous psychologist and for a decade before leaving him had felt an urgent desire to be a person in my own right – being financially independent was a contributory factor.'

Now at fifty, she owns and operates one of the most successful up-market estate agencies in London. Well-heeled in her own right, happily remarried, she is outspoken about the implications of being born an entrepreneur. How she stumbled into the high-stakes world of estate agency is a story that amuses Jan tremendously. Much of what she has to say should be quite inspirational to other women.

How did Jan first become an estate agent?

'Completely by accident. I was introduced to my original employer, who was dealing in property back in the very early Seventies, when we were on holiday and our children were playing together on the beach in Spain. We were considering buying a holiday home and he felt I had a "nose" for property and suggested that I did some buying and selling on his behalf – up to a tune of £100,000.

'Not really knowing anything about it, I went round the Hampstead estate agents with my children in tow, dressed for success in a sundress! To my amazement, one or two took me seriously and, when I called to suggest he view a house he threw out the challenge and asked why I thought he might "buy a dog and bark himself?" He gave me the name of his lawyers asking how far wrong I could be: he trusted me. So I took the bull by the horns and bought the £27,000 Golders Green house which we happily sold for £32,000 a week later. I was on my way. The relationship ended unceremoniously – luckily untraumatically because during the Seventies' property crash there were no deals around any more – but the work bug and the money buzz had infected me by that time.

'I came from a very proper middle-class family, from that ilk of people who regarded themselves as county. They had high standards and would have preferred their daughters not to work. More likely they would go to finishing school or perhaps learn Japanese flower arranging. But I was always a trouble-maker, the type who was threatened with expulsion from her boarding school. I escaped the domestic claustrophobia by securing a place at University College Hospital, London, to train as a nurse. I felt a need to acquire an insurance policy for life and to do something socially useful.

'Perhaps surprisingly to outsiders, it was a life that I loved; I worked hard right through the course and after qualification I became a casualty Charge Nurse until classically I married a hospital consultant (twenty

92

years older than myself) and produced two children. In between times, I also did some work for various publishers which provided some extra money.

'When my second child was only two years old, I discovered I had cancer. That led to a very bad three-year period, when at first I felt very depressed. I was twenty-seven, already quite unemployable, and feeling unwell with a husband who no longer fancied me. My self-confidence was at its lowest ebb, but luckily I was angry that this had happened. It was lonely: in those days no-one discussed cancer with the patient and I felt obliged to try and hide my problems for fear of being "written off". Happily the anger gave me the impetus to pick up the pieces and grab whatever life would offer in a positive light. And that was when I met the man on the beach in Spain! He had confidence in me: in many ways he saved my life. Buying those houses was not a job as such. I was on commission, it was just my first attempt to get back on my feet. When the property market dried up, I briefly felt miserable. My marriage was not going well. I was bored, broke and frustrated at home with two fabulous young children and a history of cancer, so once more I found myself accepting a challenge with no background training.

'For three years, I set up and ran an agency business working as a bulk confectionery and licorice importer. The idea emanated from another social contact. Surprisingly in retrospect, I bought a company off the shelf, and set myself up as a trader, working by phone literally from the kitchen table. If I had to meet a client, I would say I lived out of town and so we'd hold our business meeting in the calm of the coffee lounge at the Churchill Hotel.

'But I learned some useful lessons during my sugar phase. I exhibited at the World Sugar Fair in Cologne, and when asked about my previous employment, I told them without blushing that I had been in discreet Market Advisory Services. They would pretend they knew all about me! What one has to realize is that bullshit is two-sided. When contemplating whom to target, I decided they had to be in the middle of the market: medium-sized customers thankfully shy away from deep questioning in the hope that they will be thought to be at the top. One earns peanuts from small people who ask all sorts of questions, and those at the top would know I was a nobody. A certain degree of success came when I managed to get the parent company in Holland to buy me out, just in time to beat a currency fluctuation which might have destroyed my business.'

The break-up of her marriage eventually led Jan to a fiercer determination to set up some solid work for herself. Despite her obvious interest in houses – and her family's recent move to a wreck of a house in Hampstead – the renovation of which she personally master-minded working as the building contractor, hiring in outside services – she still was not able to envisage herself moving into the property business for real.

'Various people, including the man who five years later became my husband, would ask me to help them find houses, because they knew that I had my nose to the ground in Hampstead. By now, it was the late Seventies and the market was picking up again. I'd do some hunting and if I found them a place, they'd show their gratitude with champagne or roses. But I had begun to feel disgruntled. The money had run out again and I still had no real depth of experience behind me.

'However, the motivation was there, because I knew it was only a matter of time before I'd leave my husband. We had been together over twenty years and his retirement was in sight, so I had to have my own income. Then I was introduced to a younger woman, who was currently working for one of the local estate agencies. She also wanted to start up her own company. I had the courage, but no agency background. She had the track record. We had lunch together, and the brave girl went straight back to the agency and handed in her notice.

'Then we faced true terror. We had decided to invest £1,000 each of our own money. We found premises: the back room of an office; bought an off-the-shelf company; rushed to get stationery printed and debated the name under which we would trade.

'In a light-heartedly innocent mood my partner came up with "Foreign & Residential Tenancies" as she was intent on doing rentals – but it abbreviated to FART! We were determined not to use our own names, which were altogether too female and limiting to employees, and we shouldn't be anything twee like "Primrose . . . " (the office was in Primrose Hill). We had to sound imposing and grand. In haste we settled for Foreign and Residential Estates.'

But how do you set up an agency from scratch? Surely there are certain insurmountable problems?

'We dealt with every detail as it arose and seemed to hit the right tone almost by accident. The first day we had no phone and it was clearly essential. In those days, one had to wait forever to get a new line put in. But in desperation we managed to get connected to an E-line with the help of a friendly client (an emergency line for doctors and their kind) while we waited for our own phones to be put in. E-lines are ex-directory, not for the likes of estate agents, but it was a game of survival and it meant we were in touch with the public, even if they couldn't find us in the directory. We used this frustrating time as a PR joke.

94

'But one thing I had was a strong instinct to go after free editorial publicity in the absence of spare funds for circulars or advertisements, and we did get several write-ups. Miraculously they printed our address and phone number and managed to make us sound very exclusive. In response to queries about how an estate agency could be ex-directory, I would say that we were a very small company, and could not handle all the business if we were available to the public at large. We were tied up servicing our on-going clients. We lied our way out of the difficulty to generate interest and survive.

'Indeed, we were amazingly snooty and it worked. I remember one occasion, very early on, when we decided that to be open over Christmas would be a struggle, so we would close up for a month. We ran a large advertisement in the local newspaper declaring this fact. "Foreign and Residential Estates sends seasonal greetings to all its clients and associates and will be closed for the month of December." It is unheard of for estate agents to close for long and competitors sniggered, but clients came to our rescue and defended our position.

'To get started? We each took our address books and rang everyone in them; generally hustled and went out looking at properties. For the first three months, we did not pay ourselves. We had quite a few articles printed as we were two women running their own estate agency, unusual in the Seventies. The trick was to sell journalists an angle, and not make it look as though we were touting for business.

'Then, I had a real coup by writing a letter to someone in government, analysing the housing market, and pointing out that the aggregate reinstatement value to Arabs of many of the larger converted residences in prime locations was greater than the potential realization of luxury conversions for Europeans. It was just prior to the Arab investment spree in London. I never actually posted that letter to the minister in question, but I sent off a copy to the *Financial Times*, where it was printed, verbatim. I signed myself Chairman of Foreign & Residential Estates. They ran our address *and* phone number and it was a turning-point. People assumed we were an established authority and so we acquired credibility.

'After about three years, I had divorced, and was now remarried, settled down and quite happy. My young partner decided she wanted to go off and run her own business, so we parted company. When I was setting up on my own, we fought over who would keep the name, and in the end agreed we would both take new company names. Determined to sound professional and international, as I was still aiming towards the right sort of market, I became Grosvenor International.

'As Foreign & Residential Estates we had grown and by then had two freelance assistants working with us who subsequently started

their own property business. Our clients may not have had negotiators with a long property experience working for them, but they
did receive tremendous hard work and diligence, combined with a
wealth of sophisticated life experience from us. (All our negotiators
came from other sectors of the business world). We were street-wise
tough negotiators. To my mind, buying and selling is a sport. It's a bit
like playing real-life Monopoly. I just set out to get the best possible
deal for my clients – and made sure I did, whether buying or selling.

'I was used to working hard. My children were then young teenagers
and at first I certainly did not have the money for a housekeeper. I'd
often be up late into the night cleaning and ironing. Or, I'd go into
work at 7 a.m. so I could be home to cook the evening meal.

'There is always so much to do with setting up one's own business:
preparing the advertisements, doing the PR, sending out bills, keeping
the filing up to date, and mountains upon mountains of paperwork to
get through. Also one has to follow all the newspapers and magazines
to see what properties are around, and make sure one's ear is to the
ground for the sort of prices being fetched. But it was good experience,
seat-of-the-pants learning for me.'

What makes Jan and her estate agency different from any others in direct competition?

Jan has already implied that she is the type who *has* to make her own
decisions, who not only plunges in where others might not dare, but
that when she does so it seems to be unerringly the right thing to do.
She is also quite emphatic about the style of company she runs. At
first, she put it that she is, and always has been, quite an eccentric.
But then, pushed further, she admits to being an outright natural born
entrepreneur.

'From an association with Omega Management Consultants as a non-
executive director, I learned much about my profile as a worker. I
am a high achiever, who needs to be in control. I enjoy working
with people and make strong friendships, but I am perceived as
something of a loner. Basically I am unemployable. I've since learned
that the people whom I employ ideally are very pro-active with strongly
entrepreneurial or managerial drives. They would be overpowering in
a large agency, but I need independent people who are capable of
generating and executing deals with personal freedom, but within a
tightly managed office. Most estate agents are card-shufflers. But we
work with a self-selected group of clients, who are interesting and
successful people. I've been known to reject both staff and potential
clients, if I just don't feel I could work with them even if they have
reached the top.

96

'Currently we have reduced down to six people at Grosvenor. By accident we were all women until recently. The woman-only angle, particularly as I had a male office cleaner, was great fodder for the journalists. When the Suzy Lamplugh tragedy happened, we were featured in the *Daily Mail* under the title, "What the girls at risk say." Because of the style and level of our business, with an absence of "bread-and-butter" work, and the fact that we know and have chosen or had referred most of our clients, we do not feel particularly at risk. Statistically men are more likely than women to be molested: I feel this little acknowledged fact demonstrates how fear is the friend of vulnerability. Caution is imperative, but we do not feel specially vulnerable. As I said, we are choosy about our clients.'

Women in the property market tend to opt for handling residential lettings or management. How was it that Jan fitted so easily into the more male, and presumably, more aggressive world of sales?

'There are many more women today acting as sales agents, besides myself. And a few who also run their own businesses. To some degree, it might be to do with social pressures. If you are not the boss, then you can leave at 5 p.m. and go home. Maybe we should also consider the likelihood that many male bosses have not really wanted to end up in that position, they were just pressured into it by the needs of supporting a family. I was strongly motivated among other things to produce a good income for my family. My second husband is a property developer. As a woman, I do still come across the attitude that other people assume I'm the wealthy wife *playing* at being an estate agent.

'Far from it. The partnership with my property developer husband is of course very beneficial. The positive side is that, when appropriate, clients view us as a team. However, we treat each other absolutely professionally, charge each other fees and rental for use of property. But only recently, at a social function, a woman lawyer I have known for years asked me if I was still working? I turned the question back on her and said, "Yes, are you?" There can always be that level of bitchiness between women. Not only am I determined to keep up an effective and excellent service, but to uphold standards of decency: to this end I took the Estate Agency examinations eight years ago and am now a Fellow of the National Association of Estate Agents.'

But let me ask the question, as a wealthy wife why *does* Jan keep up the struggle with working?

'Because I love it! I only work because I thoroughly enjoy doing so. I enjoy the company of colleagues who are successful, motivated, lateral-thinking people. I'm good with my employees, offering them packages that suit their personal needs or lifestyle. I pay highly. Certain members of my staff work more on a commission basis, others more on a salary basis. One or two can be accommodated part-time, on the relocation side; in effect they are operating as self-employed people.'

Now, in the current economic climate, Jan is proud to admit that *they* are not losing money, while all around her estate agencies are closing their shutters and taking down the glossy ads from their windows. To what does she attribute her success?

'I couldn't really give you figures, but our turnover runs into several million pounds per year. Because of the nature and way our work is structured, we probably were not making as much profit as other agencies, when times were good, but by the same token, now times are bad we are cushioned by loyal clients at the top of the market who are in the black. We might be here working twelve-hour days, it is certainly more of a struggle, but we are surviving. Most estate agents are currently in the red. To us, it's a small business and it's *our* money. We don't want to lose anything. I was shocked recently to hear an estate agent I know well, who runs a small office in North London, saying, "Thank God, we kept our losses down to under a quarter of a million this quarter"! As far as I'm concerned, the day we go into the red, if the debt is not directly covered by the fees due to come in, then I'll take the sign down and give up.

'In the last fifteen years, we have seen the socially acceptable side of being an entrepreneur. It's no longer a dirty word! I think that being a housewife is in fact an excellent training for running a business. Which is one of the factors which explains why so many women are doing really well in the business world. One learns the self-discipline, the fact that if there is no money in the purse one cannot buy tomorrow's dinner. Women tend to lack the self-confidence simply to push themselves further, and acquire the management and jargon roles necessary.'

What about the perks of the trade? After all, Jan's diligence and skill have brought her financial freedom. Does she feel like an independently rich woman?

'For a short time, I was driving around in my ex-husband's green Porsche, wondering if this was the self-image I'd been waiting to create. But then I felt uncomfortable with it, and have since changed to a more boring, black Daimler. I think the image of oneself portrayed by one's car is very complex, especially for a woman. It all depends on how one envisages oneself. Now, I've opted for the image of being unostentatious, indulgent, but ultimately comfortable – if you're driving around most of the day you should be able to enjoy a few of life's comforts, shouldn't you?'

Facts:
Staff: Currently 6 people.
Turnover: Difficult to quantify. Millions may change hands, or not. More importantly, we still manage to trade in the black.

Chapter Four

THE DOGGEDLY
INDEPENDENT STREAK

WHAT ARE THE reasons women cite for leaving paid employment to set up their own business? Natural independence. A refusal to be defeated at work, or to be kept back by men who may appear more experienced, but probably just won't give up any of their power. The unknown force that comes from having children, which interrupts a career and may make one look again at values, priorities and what one wants from life. Youthfulness, ambition, not caring about status as bestowed by the normal corporate or hierarchical structures of the world.

But on top of these is there, I kept wondering, not a hidden quality that adds up to the true entrepreneurial streak? Or, in the case of women business owners, more so than of comparable men, does it often come back to social factors such as those listed above? Is it a question of a blend of the two?

Sometimes, when interviewing the feisty, daring and usually self-confident women for this book, I began to doubt that they, in any way, had been *forced* out. Most of these women do seem to be naturals. They may say to me, with a touch of self-deprecation: 'I'm pretty much unemployable'. But one has to ask, is that said in criticism or perhaps self-congratulation? To be an employer, rather than an employee, puts one in a position of control, the person whom governments admire; the type of person whom we look up to with envy and pride.

To some degree, I do think that women are helped in their entrepreneurial endeavours by their very lack of a history of success in the corporate world. Their predecessors tend to have been married women, content to live through a man's life and work. Their compatriots maybe are struggling for corporate success, bumping their heads against the glass ceiling. There is less a feeling of being at complete risk, that failure of a business venture would be the end of the world. Perhaps that very freedom from fear is what helps drive women on. There is no conformity, no set pattern to fit, not too much shame in having to admit to friends or foes that it hasn't quite worked out as you had dreamed.

Interestingly, the women in this section whether single, married, or divorced, also tend to be the type of women who look after themselves and their families. There is no hint of any of these women being able to rest on their laurels. They are the breadwinners. That same need to be in control at home, obviously spills over into the business life, too; it taps into the same source of energy and pride in oneself.

The three women featured here are in different forms of businesses, though, as is so common with women, all are in service industries: one is in financial planning, the second in training for managers and women returners, and the third in recruitment. All three run small- to medium-sized companies, with a healthy turnover and decent-sized staff. All take a fierce pride in the way they run these businesses believing that, as women, they have something very positive to offer in the ways of management and organization that others might even envy.

Mary Robert

FIONA PRICE
Fiona Price and Partners:
financial advisers to business
and professional women

VERY FEW PEOPLE start their own business on leaving school, college
or graduating with a degree. It is more traditional to work for a few
years, build up a level of expertise, competence and good contacts;
only then might you feel brave enough to launch out on your own.
Fiona Price is one of those very rare people who became immediately
self-employed at the age of twenty-three and shortly afterwards she
set up her own business.

She became a financial adviser which was unusual even in her
own terms, though it was a growing, flourishing trade at the time.
Since those early years, Fiona, now aged thirty-one, has very much
arrived in the market-place with a well-respected, often talked-about
company, that specializes in giving financial advice to professional
women. Three years ago she was awarded a *Cosmopolitan* magazine
Young Entrepreneurs Award.

Why did Fiona consider running her own business?
'I came into financial services in 1983, straight from a psychology
degree which I'd followed up with an MBA. It actually came as
a complete surprise to me that I went into the world of finance,
because I had always been scared stiff of figures. I remember at
sixteen struggling through maths O level; in my degree, and even

in the MBA, I felt that I must be the only student emerging who did not fully understand a balance sheet.

'But what I did acquire from Business School was a strong sense that I was *unemployable*. I just could not see myself as part of a big bureaucracy, nor the corporate culture, where decision making would be slow and my creativity would be stunted. I needed to find something that would allow me a fair degree of freedom. I just happened to stumble across one of those crass advertisements for financial services that were running at the time.

'The main appeal to me was that here was an area into which I could come in fresh, where I could create my own client base, from which I would earn an income dependent on my results, i.e. from commission. But I would nevertheless have the back-up and support of a very large organization to get me going.

'As far as a potential career, it was the *people* side that most appealed. I liked the idea of being able to solve problems and help improve people's lives. I have always seen financial planning as a very creative science. It is all about people skills, understanding their needs (almost through osmosis), and coming up with solutions. The theoretical numbers' side is really far less important. And that led me to feel that I would overcome my fear of numbers.

'However, at the age of twenty-three, having only ever been a student, not only was I wet behind the ears, in terms of never having been employed, but I was setting myself a very hard task going self-employed from day one. Maybe one of the hardest parts was that I could never see myself as a salesman. Even my father told me he was horrified that I would become a "life insurance salesman"! From the very beginning, therefore, I worked hard to persuade people that I was a professional and very service-oriented – albeit that I was working in the midst of a very sales-oriented group of colleagues. And, of course, the sales side was the reputation the business already owned.

'I had to build up my client list from friends and contacts, because I just would not do cold-calling. By working hard and delivering on my service-based concept, I did very well quickly, and soon was one of their top producers/salespersons. Within two years I had set up a new office for them, recruiting twelve people.

'Then I began to get itchy feet and wanted to move on. They were a pyramid-based sales organization, and they were ceasing to be independent in the market-place. Eventually, I decided to resign and to set up my own business. I went in at first with a partner, and we set up *Modern Money* in 1986; giving ourselves one month just before Christmas, in the middle of a British Telecom strike, to do the logistics of setting up a business: finding office space, organizing the stationery, and raising £25,000 which we needed for our launch. As I was unproven in terms of a business, I could not go to the banks for a loan. So I turned to people I knew, and in the end all the money came from a client.'

Had Fiona learned the 'logistics of running a business' on the MBA course?

'No, the only information I had absorbed was from my limited experience of working with that company for three years. I found that the general problems such as leases, and phone systems, you have to learn as you go along and that you do make mistakes. My partner was meant to be responsible for the financial aspect of the company but, after just over a year, we went our separate ways. I felt we could no longer work together as we were moving in completely different directions. He bought out my share of the business, and that enabled me to go off and set up on my own. By then, I was branching out with the intention of advising professional women; an interest that had grown over the past few years since becoming involved with women's business networks and so often being asked for my advice.'

Why was it so new to be offering financial advice to women?
'As a company, all the marketing and PR we put out is aimed primarily at women, and basically at those living in the South East who are working, with an income between £20,000 and £45,000. They are usually between the ages of twenty and fifty, single or married, though the majority tend to be unmarried and without children (but, of course, many are in relationships).

'What I have discovered is that even high-powered business women have a block about money and figures, partly because they have no ready frame of reference. Until recently, women were not used to earning such amounts of money or, if they had money, they would let it be handled by their husbands (or the bank, or their father). Women who have careers and families very often think of themselves last. All their energies go out towards others.

'I also knew that women need flexibility written into any financial arrangements for themselves, because they may take a career break for children, they marry or are divorced. Even men should think along those same lines, now, as they may take a few years off for family or, for example, to study an MBA. Planning for a woman's finances may be less concerned with the *figures*, than with her priorities and potential resources.'

Does Fiona think women have so often ignored the financial side of their lives, because they prefer to wait until the mythical man comes along to sort it all out?

'Too many women still ignore the issue of money in a relationship. They blind themselves with faith and optimism that they will be looked after. We're British, we can talk about sex, politics and religion, but not about money! Recently I have written about women and divorce. Do you know very few women realize that while married they have been part of their husband's pension scheme. But, if they get divorced without any provision being made to share in that pension, if they have been non-working mothers now trying to get back into the work-place, (say in their forties), then they will lose out tremendously on potential pensions. Solicitors handling divorce don't even point this out. And too many women end up on the poverty line in late middle age. Conversely, busy professional women put their families and their careers in front of their personal affairs, quite often, including their finances, so we ensure that while it isn't top of their list of priorities, it's top of ours.'

So how does she help women overcome these problems?

'We're an all-female team and we understand our market very well. We know that women are often less confident in this area, that they demand excellent service, and they understand that financial planning is best applied over the long term because situations in a woman's life can change at any time. She may marry, she may have children, she may divorce or break up with a partner.

'We see our clients every six months or more often if necessary. We help them understand their finances and to take charge of their lives. In recent years, there has been a lot of direct marketing to women, because the financial world woke up to the presence of a new consumer: woman. But their attitude just seems to me to have been saying: "How can we improve our sales figures this month?" They're not really thinking of women's needs. They'll do some research and then market a product specifically to women, but it is not really geared to helping them.

'Most women (most people for that matter) are not sufficiently well-informed to be able to discriminate between all the products on the market. What they tend to do is follow up on a mailshot here or there, or take out a scheme that appeals. When they come to us we discover a fragmented basket of policies. The good news is that now women are realizing they have to do something. The bad news is that they have been hard-sold, do not understand what they have got and why, and few of their pension, life insurance, or savings policies dovetail or synchronize. Nor will it help them achieve any long-term goals. Mostly we find it best to leave what is there in place, and to build on it to create firm foundations. One thing we show is that you cannot have *control* over your money, and therefore over your life, until you understand what choices you have. This is why it is so important to work with a professional, impartial financial adviser.'

Is there a reason why more women are now seeking Fiona's help?
'Independent taxation has made women much more aware and forced them to discuss with their husbands just what the financial situation of the family might be. Then, there are increasing numbers of women becoming self-employed, and increasing divorce statistics. All these things are starting to make people realize it is not the *kiss of death* to begin to take control of your finances. People are also understanding that you can hang on to financial independence within a relationship.'

What else makes Fiona Price different to other financial advisers?

'We're unusual in that we are remunerated partly from fees and partly from commission. I don't think it would be acceptable for us to earn solely from commission. If we end up being generous with our time and no business was created, then we'd lose out. Or, if we worked solely on commission then we might be unethically promoting contracts simply because they would pay us a higher return. We want to be truly independent of the companies selling policies.

'To that end, we are both fee-based and commission-based. We can cover our bases and retain our independence. Although we see our clients once every six months, they have access to us within that time. We charge them a quarterly fee, on a sliding scale dependent on their income level. It is quite affordable; for example, on an income of not more than £25,000 a year, we charge £35 a quarter. If we make a recommendation for, say, a pension or life insurance policy, then we would normally receive a commission, too, from that company. Or, if we opted for one paying no commission, then we could charge the client an arrangement fee.

'Women are discerning clients and I think they are amenable to this type of balance. They are keen on the fact we retain independence from the big finance companies and they know that good sense costs money. Our client base is currently about 70 per cent female, whereas the average financial advisers would have at most 5–10 per cent female. Of the remainder, I would say that 10 per cent are married couples and 20 per cent are men, very often recommended by our female clients.

'But, because it is relatively new to be charging fees, in our business, we are particularly keen that our terms-of-business letter lays out all our charges in black and white. Even solicitors and accountants don't do that. Why? Because they haven't really thought through what it is they are offering the client. As I see it, we are at present climbing the learning curve in terms of educating our clients.'

How did Fiona get the business launched?

'I began with just one member of staff and myself. And at the beginning, obviously, I had to be a jack of all trades: advising, organizing the company, and working on strategy to develop. We're a limited company, I'm the majority shareholder and there are three directors now. My "partners" are more like associates. We operate an open-house, shared decision-making style of working. The people who work with me develop their own skills and talents in different ways and I encourage that.

'The directors are all on salaries, but everyone else works on a profit share. I have definitely learned that it is impossible to delegate until you yourself understand the business inside out. There really are no short cuts. You also need to surround yourself with the right people. You cannot do everything yourself, of course, but you should never ignore problems in the hope they will go away.'

And how does she go about attracting new clients?

'I do all the PR myself. Because we were such a niche business, and I sensed from the beginning that it would appeal to the media, I targeted our business directly at the financial journalists and women's interest magazines. It was our mission statement to develop financial planning and take it out to Britain's business and professional women, so I had to create a high profile. I have learned a lot along the way. For example, if your story is of interest the first time round, you have to build on journalists' respect, you have to work on a relationship with them. They will turn to me now for article ideas or for quotes. I am careful to be helpful in the broadest sense, not just push my own business, because I need long-term coverage.

'A lot of people starting out like I did might have no idea how to contact the media, but I just began with a basic primitive press release and worked from gut instinct. If the newspaper or magazine did not respond immediately, I found that they would file it away, and then slowly would follow up. Now I meet with the financial journalists regularly and help them focus on good stories. In theory, I'm here with my finger on the pulse. I'm a good resource.'

So how does she keep abreast with all the changing financial legislation and products available? Fiona grins.

'It is not easy. We have to absorb all the new information for our clients. The technical director has to be *au fait* with all the new

110

changes. But we share the reading of journals and meet regularly to pool information. At our technical briefing meetings we discuss new developments.'

And how does she attract new clients? Surely there are limits to the numbers of well-heeled professional women out there?

'We give a lot of financial seminars, for women's organizations, newspapers and magazines such as *Company* and *New Woman* and through the networks. We also do mailshots. Now, my particular role is almost entirely involved with marketing, PR, systems and strategy for the business as well as looking after my clients (though I personally am not in a position to take on any more clients). Because I'm very much a people-first type, I find myself naturally attracted to PR and to working with the media. Probably, I could have had a career in either of those fields too. I'm not really a technical person.

'My main aim by the end of this year is that we should be the one name on the lips of our prospective clients. Already we are quite well known, it is just a question of keeping the ball rolling. I write articles and columns for magazines such as *Company* and *Woman's Journal*, and give talks on finance programmes on LBC, and on Thames TV, Women's Hour, etc. Then there are the seminars I do in conjunction with the *Daily Mail* and the *Guardian* – on women and money. Seminars are a very good way of attracting new clients, as you are meeting people in an easy and non-threatening way.'

I wanted to know whether Fiona gives advice to women on running their own businesses as she was sounding so shrewd?

'Only if I am asked! From my own standpoint I'd say it is important that you know your market through and through, and that you work back from that point of view. Your business must reflect in all ways the service you aim to provide. You need to go through each stage of the process and be able to define it: the service you provide and your in-house style. These are all your selling points.'

So what is her style?

'Offering the highest possible standard of service, and being practical, approachable, non-jargon oriented. To make sense in people's lives. To help them remain in control of their lives.

'Women must recognize that life is less predictable than ever before. Relationships may be transitory, so women need to be in control and not be threatened by money or ignore it. Women owe it to themselves

111

to be confident, to be in control of their own money, to take stock and come to terms with financial matters.'

Does Fiona plan to grow the company or is she happy remaining relatively small?

'Oh, no. I want it to become a fairly significant company over the next two or three years. One lesson on running a small business I've had to absorb myself can be seen in the fact we have had to move offices three times in four business years. We began in two rooms, moved to one floor and have just taken on a whole building in Covent Garden where we intend to stay. The reason we have had such short-term premises is that the only way a small business can afford Central London rents, is to take on a short lease, outside the Landlord and Tenant Act. Then it is just about affordable. We have to be central for clients to get in to see us, during or just before or after their working day.'

What are Fiona's own plans?

'At some point I would like to be less involved in the business. I want to write a book, and I'd like to do some work in TV. I'll leave myself open to possibilities. Also, I see myself taking up some non-executive directorships. First, I want this company to realize its potential, to reach a certain breadth and depth.'

Would she be bought out?

'I don't know. Who can tell what I would say if the offer came up? But it hasn't come to that yet. That might be an option, or maybe I'd prefer to work here on a three-day week basis, so I could still do other things. I have every confidence in my future, however it turns out.'

Facts:
Staff: 7 financial advisers and 3 administrative people.
Turnover: Not in figures, but they have around 1000 clients.

Jim Rice Photography

LINDA STOKER
Dow-Stoker: management and
women returner training

Do WOMEN TURN to their own businesses because they feel forced out of the male corporate world, because they just don't fit, or because they know they will never progress beyond a certain level? Do they opt to go out on their own because having children creates a natural break in their career path, and they find it hard to slip back in? Or, do they go it alone because deep down they are such strong individualists, true entrepreneurs by nature, that somehow instinct tells them they would no longer be satisfied as someone else's employee?

Linda Stoker is one such woman. You could read any of the above reasons into her decisions in life. Head of a company that specializes in management training, and in more recent years, specifically in training courses for Women Returners, Linda is still only in her mid thirties. She has two young daughters, and appears to keep up the juggling of an enormous portfolio of business successes, with private achievements, all at the same time.

Like many women, Linda is also disarmingly frank and honest; she will confess that running such a big business is often a major headache. Yet she could never return to being 'small' again; that would not hold enough excitement any more. At least this way, life is an adventure.

In recent years, Linda has developed a high profile for herself, skilfully promoting particularly her Women Returners' courses through the media, writing books, and making many television appearances. Two books have been published by Bloomsbury this year, *Having It All* and *The Women Returners' Guide*. A few months ago, *Good Housekeeping* magazine voted her 'Woman of the Month', and described her as the 'patron saint of women returners'.

Why did Linda start the business?

'I came out of a long career in marketing, personnel and training in the hotel and catering industry. I was used to training staff in companies at the industry level and at national level through the (then) Manpower Services Commission. Yet, I knew that within these organizations, they would never let me through to director level. And I just was not satisfied to stay at mid-management level. My biggest problems were threefold: being working class, too young, and female!

'Although I'd been to grammar school and went on to college for A levels, I came from the type of family that didn't believe in sending a girl to university. My mother wanted me to do a secretarial course with office skills. Her idea of success would be for me to serve as a managing director's PA. I suppose the keyboard skills came in useful, as I do a lot of my own writing at the word processor now.

'However, there came a point where I no longer felt I was working to my full potential. And I began to wonder what to do next? I'd been married for eight years and the one thing I hadn't done was have a child. So I came off the Pill one day, and a few days later was pregnant. It came as rather a shock. I gave up working for a while, and decided to start my own business. In those days, that meant basically being self-employed, working as a freelancer. I was invited to write some booklets, and found I could work and bring the baby along with me. Then I was given the opportunity of joining some other consultants to write a training programme for IBM. That boosted my confidence.

'The freelance work began to mushroom beyond my expectations. I had begun by working from home, with a neighbour looking after the baby part-time. And I did think that if I could do so well only working part-time, I should go full-time and hire someone to look after the child permanently. Then the Manpower Services Commission asked me to run some courses for women returners. I have to admit at first to being very snooty about the idea. Who wanted to be training just women? But an incredible thing happened. I entered a roomful of shy women, who had all been out of the workplace for a few years looking after children, and discovered that they were an incredibly talented, interesting bunch. They had tons of ability, what they lacked was self-confidence. And so I found my vocation. To a degree, I was just like them, though I had not cut myself off so abruptly from the work world. I sympathized, but mostly found them great fun to work with.

'Things were going along well, business doing nicely, when suddenly I became pregnant again. That brought my whole world to a standstill. I remember driving off into the night, crying because it would mean the end of my business, that I couldn't stand being at home with babies all day long. What would I do?

'I tried advertising for an au pair. But it's funny, being working class, you don't think of yourself as the type who hires nannies. I imagined they were for the aristocracy. A young student came to see me, she'd left college and needed some childcare experience to get on a course. She was keen to work full-time as a nanny. I had to laugh at the idea of me having a nanny. I told her I couldn't afford to pay very much, but she wanted the job. It was just what I needed. She created the space for me in which to work, I found more clients, and the business began to take off. Six and half years later, she is still with us. Now she is officially the Dow-Stoker nanny, looks after all the company children, takes care of the school-age ones in the holidays, does work in the office too, and has a company car.'

But how do you make a company grow, I was interested? Rather as with Penny Phipps in the PR business, Linda has moved from being a freelancer, bringing in enough work to cover expenses and make a profit, to running a small- to medium-sized business.

'The first big decision was to take on a part-time secretary and to decide that I was going to be responsible for her livelihood. The first person I took on was another woman returner who wanted part-time work, just two mornings a week. But I can tell you, that led to some sleepless nights! Could I afford her? I went ahead and created an office out of a downstairs room at home. Eventually she became full-time, and was doing all my administration. We then brought in a YTS, sixteen-year-old trainee, sending him for one day a week to a local college to take a business course (BTech). He's still with us too. Gradually, we took on more and more staff as we grew. Each time it would be when we reached the point of just not being able to cope any more. Yet, at the same time, I never stopped thinking: "Oh, no, another wage to pay!" We have since moved into lovely office space, in a converted mill just near my home on the Hertfordshire/Essex border.'

How did Linda bring in enough work to keep on growing?

'I began by going round all my old contacts, or recommendations and leads. Once I have the "in", I find I'm OK. It all comes down to being really *determined*, constantly ringing people, making appointments, following up on the day you've agreed. You just can never stop. I have a diary full of lists of people to call back. I'm a good saleswoman, I suppose.'

This led me to another question, that had begun to intrigue me about the entrepreneurial type. Does the main impulse of the business come from her? Can anyone else sell Linda's business for her as well as Linda herself?

'Really, my success comes from my contacts, yes. But then if I employed sales people they could steal my business. That happens all the time, and there is very little you can do about it through the courts. So you do have to be careful. My individual strength is in selling and marketing the business. I have developed good personal relationships. Business is all about trust. You have to feel you get along with someone, you need to find customers who are almost like friends. The pay-off is that you'll enjoy your work much more.

'We're in a niche market, I accept. But we are certainly not alone out there, though maybe we are the best known in the field of women returners. So far we've trained 3,000 women to go back to work, linked with several of the major companies in the country. We're a sizeable company now, for a service business. Most of my team of consultants, who work for me part-time on a freelance basis, are women returners, who prefer to remain self-employed. But something goes well between us, because they are all very loyal.'

Did Linda intend her company to become this big?
'I was happy when I was a freelancer, but then it just started to grow and I was not going to prevent that progress. One day I remember coming home and I wrote myself a target. I just wrote down £100,000, and decided to go for that figure in a year. I also drafted out a marketing plan. All that came out of anger, because a business man I knew had been very unprofessional and that incensed me. In fact, I hit £150,000 in my third year of business. And from there we just kept developing and growing.

'Apart from the women returners' courses, we provide management, supervisory and personnel development training, for over one hundred companies. Although major companies have their own internal trainers, we have teams of consultants, which include psychologists and counsellors, who have specific skills. So we can tap into whatever type of trainer a company needs. I have taken many courses myself over the years. But it's quite a game, in that we have to stay at the front of the market. We have to charge competitively and make sure we're always abreast of new ideas and material. Training is also a great field for people pinching each other's ideas. So, if you invent any technique for your courses, you can guarantee it quickly be copied elsewhere.'

What next? Does Linda intend to make the company even bigger?
'I've reached a difficult stage. There are problems in running a medium-sized business. You don't have the advantage of size, nor do you have the opportunity of being lean and mean as if you were very small. I could go bigger, with a takeover and become part of a plc. But I'm not sure if I want that, as that would mean my becoming an employee again. They start putting controls on you, once you're on a salary. And again I'd probably be in the position of being the only woman on the board.

'When you sell out, they look at your profit in recent years and assess its potential. You are paid an amount up-front, and some in shares. And then they give you a financial target to meet. They may say the total package is worth a million pounds, but that will be paid over three years, and you have to put your back into the work in that time to ensure you keep up the profits. They call it the "golden handcuffs".

'Personally, I've been seeking different developments. Last year, my object was to become more widely known. I have been on eight television programmes, endless radio shows and I think in every national newspaper, as well as the women's magazines. I was really pleased this year to be invited to the Woman of the Year luncheon, as a Woman of the Year!'

How does the business impinge on her personal life?
'Ah yes, well, I'm separated, a single mother, and recently I began a relationship with a new man. And I can tell you that being in that sort of unstable position personally, does not help you when you've a business to run. My other main objective is in fact to get my personal life in order. My husband and I broke up a while ago. At least I now know I can live on my own, with my girls. Yet I can also see that I'd prefer to be in a marital-type relationship again. I miss all that.

'Now I have a new boyfriend, but it is difficult building a new relationship when you have children, and when you have the problems of a business to run as well. Relationships take time and a lot of emotion. Also, I've discovered that when you get to my age, you don't meet anyone who comes without a past. They've all been damaged by former relationships. They all have some problem. So we have our ups and downs. Also, he is the type of guy who decided to opt out of the rat race. He now works as a tree surgeon. And he's having to deal with a woman running her own successful business; I thought that might be difficult for him but he manages me quite well!

119

'When a huge change comes into your life, like a marriage break-up, it makes you re-evaluate what is important to you. I'm still trying to decide. I've enjoyed writing books this year, I've enjoyed doing television presentation work. I have an enormous amount of energy, but I feel somehow that I need to find a direction. Maybe the television opportunities, the books and the business could all run hand in hand.

'What I say is that this year I have written two books, dealt with a divorce, managed the company, coped with being a single parent, and felt really pleased that my children don't seem to have suffered because they both did very well in school. But there are still more problems in sight. I might have to sell the house, because my former husband is having financial problems with his business and I may have to give him his share of the property.

'Basically, I run the whole family and pay for everything, right down to the private schools. I'm also responsible for the company, and everyone's wages there. The buck always stops with me, so I just have to keep the money coming in!'

Does she feel it is hard to be a single woman, and run her own business?

'Oh yes. It is very isolating. You might be dealing with the same people all the time. How are you going to meet someone new? I took myself to many places to meet new people, including the local gym. After all, I realized I had no idea what I liked to do in my leisure time. I'd always been married, or working very hard. I had never concentrated on me. When the recent *Good Housekeeping* magazine came out, calling me, "Woman of the Month", I remember someone saying to me: "People must be really proud of you." And I had a horrible moment of loneliness, realizing that not having a husband, there was no-one to be proud of me. My children are too young.

'There is a problem in being the one person who is always giving out, and getting no support. You do need someone in your private life, to give you loving attention, who likes you just for being *you*, not because you make money or for what you've achieved. Otherwise, you can be running with burdens all the time, there are too many responsibilities.'

Does Linda see herself as a genuine entrepreneur?
'I met a chap recently on a course in America. He was an accountant, who remembered me from when we were little kids, living on a crowded street. When he heard what I was doing today, he said, "I always knew you'd run your own business." He went on and explained that at the age of eight, when we were at primary school, the

headteacher announced one day that we'd made £90 at the school fête. I'd looked thrilled. The next day, I cleared out our garage, borrowed other people's toys, and made a lucky dip which I'd charged the other kids 3*d*. to enter. My mum was furious and made me give all my £1 10*s*. profit back. And I'd given away my brother's toys! But I had seized on an opportunity and followed it through, and that is what business is all about.

'On the other hand, if I sat down and really thought about what I am doing I might not sleep at nights. I have to find £250,000 a year to pay wages and running costs, before I even begin to make a profit. I don't spend much myself, except on the children.'

Would Linda recommend this as a way of life to other women?

'Only if it turns you on, if the thrills are enough to keep you going. I remember winning my first big contract. I was driving through London with the car radio playing, the windows down, and Sting was singing, "Everything she does is magic!" If you get that kind of high, then it is for you. But if you're the type who would worry and get ulcers from the stress, then don't touch it. Life is too short.

'I would say I have a need to be in control, so I'll always be doing something like this. I couldn't go back to being self-employed now; that would feel too small. But I won't branch out too drastically, it is best to stick to what you know.'

Facts:
Staff: 11 permanent, and 38 consultants hired on a freelance basis.
Turnover: About £750,000 p.a.

Michael Pyne

JUDY FARQUHARSON
Judy Farquharson Ltd: recruitment

ANYONE WHO HAS been looking at the job vacancy advertisements in the national newspapers, in recent years, might have spotted the name Judy Farquharson. I wonder how many suspected there was a real person behind the name? We might think that it's merely a front to attract women to the recruitment offices.

But Judy is very much a real person, a dynamic and forceful character now in her mid-fifties, who says she set up her own business by accident, somehow she felt forced into going it alone. For Judy, as we have seen in the other stories in this section, the impulse obviously came from a mixture of not feeling that she fitted into any so-called normal working scenario, that she would never be allowed to progress there, and that deep down she disapproved of their business practices. And, like Linda Stoker, Judy discovered a vocation in life: in her case to help female graduates who, certainly back in the late Sixties, were coming out of universities in their droves, but were unable to find decent careers, or employers brave enough to take them on.

Judy Farquharson has concentrated over the years on female recruitment, though now she covers both men and women equally. She deals with a fairly wide niche market covering publishing, publications, design, marketing, PR, personnel and market research.

*

123

'I started my business in 1968. I'd say it was all by sheer accident, as after years in various jobs I happened to work at a recruitment consultancy, while looking for a new job. With no training or qualifications behind me, other than a spell at art school, I had nowhere to go; in those days young women either became a secretary or they got married. I never had a bean to my name, as my father had gone off to Canada, and I'd been left alone in London with no family to support me. He even made me leave art school to go and earn a living, though I did continue classes in the evenings.

'But the recruitment agency offered me a job, and I discovered, by default, that I was quite a natural; though in my heart of hearts, I wondered if I was not pretty much unemployable. Then a job vacancy came in for a graduate to run the information department of an advertising agency. This was back in 1967. I remember running the advertisement in a newspaper, and being inundated with responses from women graduates. They would come in to see me, weeping and moaning that they could not find a job, that no-one would employ them. And there had I been imagining that having a degree was a passport to another life!

'Anyway, I was determined to do something about that situation. I'd been with the agency by then for about three years. At a party, I was telling someone that I wanted to start my own business, specializing in placing women graduates; I was sounding off loudly about the fact that, by comparison, their male counterparts had little difficulty. Historically, this was the winter of 1967–8, and no-one had yet uttered the words "Women's Lib", though it had all just begun in America.

'A business man listening told me to go ahead, that he would back me; he thought it was a great idea. The next day, he rang me to say that he had meant it (he was only an acquaintance). I was worried that maybe I could be sued for conflict of interest with my present employer. In the end, with my prevarications, he withdrew. But by then I had become keen on the idea, and felt I could find someone else to back me. I approached another contact, then with Haymarket Publishing (where young Maurice Saatchi was tied up in a broom cupboard doing tele-ad sales!), and so I went to him with my idea. He said it was brilliant and to set it up immediately.

'I found premises, did everything one has to do in two weeks: produced a marketing plan, a balance sheet, and a profit and loss forecast. I didn't have a clue how to go about any of it, but I learned pretty quickly. Roughly, I just worked it out on the basis of what I knew a placement was worth, and what I would need to earn. My husband at the time helped me through the jungle.

'And so we launched Graduate Girls, a very sexist name looking back. I was very naïve, so it took three weeks before I realized I was not running my own company, but that I was locked into Haymarket. I was on a salary made up of commission and bonus, and I most certainly was not a director. I was owned by Haymarket, and they were not going to promote me on to the board. Well, I carried on like that for four years. No-one ever invited me to board meetings. They had no idea what my business was about. But we soldiered on, attracting more and more interest for women graduates from the City in particular, where companies were taking women on at the marketing end, employing a lot of law and languages graduates.'

So what made the company grow? The answer, like so many, seems to be in skilful PR and marketing. Judy met someone at a party who promised to print a mention of the new agency in the *Observer*.

'The article was all of an inch or so long. At the time I was working from a two- to three-roomed office, with a married friend who was helping me out part-time. When I opened my doors the next Monday morning, there was a queue of women a mile long. That one article brought in 400–500 responses from women. I must have interviewed fifty on that first day. Here was all this obvious talent, and I did not have a single job on my books! Most of them were raw, straight from university. I picked one of them I liked best and asked if she would come to help me. I chose well, because she herself was a real entrepreneurial spirit, who stayed with me for two years, and now runs her own wine company.

'I turned in desperation to my previous contacts, such as the City employers. And again the response was terrific; one company took on twenty women graduates. Only one wrote back an hilarious letter saying that they would not dream of employing a woman graduate, because their place was in the home! This was in 1968, it's hard to remember that attitudes still had not changed then.

'Things were tough compared with today. For example, we'd advertise senior jobs and even then the company would ask the woman at interview if she could type. It was still unacceptable for women to work when they had children, and I certainly could never place a woman if she was pregnant. One firm actually insisted that the woman did *not* get pregnant, by making her take the Pill in front of them every day. You really cannot imagine it now, can you?'

But how did Judy go about setting up her own company, under her name?

'I was beginning to realize that I was being a fool, because I still did not own the company. I had set it up the wrong way. The trouble with me may be that money has never been a great motivator. I was pioneering something that I knew was very important. That meant more to me than money.

'That level of recruitment is not a great money-maker, because the turnover is not there. The salaries are not high enough, and we spent a lot of time and effort placing people. In recruitment, it's the high end and the low end that make money. The middle, where we come in, does not. We had to branch out into secretarial placements, as that is where the bread-and-butter work lies. I don't suppose we could have survived without secretaries, they were the one commodity in need.

'Yet we just grew and grew. From myself and half a person, we went up to a staff of ten in four years and moved to bigger premises. It was all great fun and really interesting work. I also had my two children in that period. But things changed when Haymarket announced it was about to go public. All the managers were called in to be told we had to beef up our profits. I knew what they wanted to do with Graduate Girls: make us go the way of Alfred Marks. Once we were public, they thought we should open up branches in every town. But I argued our uniqueness. We had queues of graduates on our books, but just not enough of the right type of jobs. All the time, I sensed they were plotting against me.

'Indeed, it happened as suspected, one day they suddenly swooped, changed the locks and were ready to take us over. We were going to become like Brook Street Bureau and move into the tele-ad sales market. I said, 'Over my dead body, not with my name involved'. So I was told to go, to which I agreed. I had already moved ahead of them. I'd made copies of all my client files and had taken them home with me. The ten staff members were told they could stay, with higher salaries. But they all left after being forced to work out their notice.

'So I turned around immediately and set up on my own, taking four of the previous staff with me. Judy Farquharson Ltd was set up in 1972, on an overdraft facility from the bank. Within six months we were in profit.

'But 1972, if you remember, was the end of the previous property boom. Rents were sky high. I managed to acquire offices at a pepper-corn rent, only by going under the umbrella of another company again. This time I had to promise to hand over 25 per cent of my profits. I really did not want to go that way and, in the end, was able to buy them out. Things have certainly changed a lot since those days.'

Judy Farquharson describes herself as a pioneer and is proud of the way she runs her business. There are certain values she has determinedly adhered to, and certain principles she feels are uniquely female in its management.

*

'Basically, I run my business so that it's the sort of company I would like to work in. For example, I have no-one working on commission. I don't see how you can do that, not when you're working with *people* as your commodity. In London, from the top head-hunters down, they all work on commission, but that means you might be manipulating people, and probably making no effort to place the difficult ones.

'My staff work on a salary and an equal profit-sharing basis. They also get one day off a month, in lieu of working through lunch-times. You see, I had my two young children in those early years. I was married, but was always the major breadwinner. I had a daily nanny who left at 6 p.m., and so I rushed out of the office at 5.30 p.m. every day. I would never impose working practices on someone else that I would not want myself. My children were most important to me. I'd do all the usual things in the evenings: the cooking and putting the children to bed. And my second child did not sleep through the night until he was three, whereupon I would have to get up and face running my own business. It was pretty exhausting stuff, but I know what other women go through!

'So, I arrange it that my staff work frantically hard, non-stop through lunch-times which is when many people can get in for interviews. And then they down tools and are all gone by 6 p.m. I hate the way men, in many corporations, play the "Whose going to be last out of the office" routine when they are not necessarily working.

'I do run rather a "cosy" company. I provide lunch. We cook up soup and have sandwiches from Marks & Spencer. We have a very good name and my staff are terrifically loyal. I also run things very democratically and I think women appreciate that. I have pioneered three major innovations: 1) no commissions, which leads to a much less stressful atmosphere, because you are not after each other's throats; 2) no smoking, we've been that way for about fourteen years already; and 3) c.v.s rather than application forms. When I first began in recruitment all companies had their own forms. We'd have hundreds of forms. And women never seemed to fit them, particularly if they'd been out of work for a few years; or often there'd be questions like, "When did you do your National Service?" C.v.s are a better tool to show your personality, they give you a feel for the person.

'We tend to be all female here. I'm the ancient crone! Now we have one man who has joined us, it must be hard on him to be surrounded by women. If one of my staff has a baby, they may leave, or return part-time, or we do job-shares. I know such things still upset people in other companies, but I have to stick by my own principles.'

*

Looking back, what would Judy see as the most positive side to running her own company?

'It's been great fun. I've been able to manipulate for my own ends. My children were able to be paramount in my life, and yet I could continue working and be fulfilled. I've always been pretty much a pioneer. I was forty when I had the last baby, and he's sixteen years old now. I suppose I've lived and worked through many of the great changes of the last decade.'

Facts:
Staff: 14.
Turnover: A little over £1 million.

Part Two

WHERE TO GO NEXT

Chapter Five

STAYING SMALL:
THE POSITIVE APPROACH

SOME VERY PERSONAL decisions have to be made by any woman contemplating setting up her own business. What size of business does
she have in mind? Is visible success, growth, planned expansion,
responsibility for employees' pay and welfare, perhaps even personal
wealth, of importance in her plans? If not, is she sure that her decision
is the right one, because the alternative is likely to mean a rather
low-profile career more on the self-employed or freelance lines?

There are many women, indeed, who are quite simply more comfortable with 'small' concerns, who prefer to stay in work at what they love
best, not to divest their energies, nor expand their ideas too widely.
The hundreds of thousands of the self-employed pay justice to that
concept: the women who earn a sufficient living to keep themselves
and their families happy, whether that involves cleaning other people's
houses, doing some childcare, selling home-crafted goods, or maybe
doing word-processing and typing from computers at home.

However, the women profiled in this section are definitely in
business. They could not be categorized as part of the army of
self-employed. Their individual decision has been *not* to employ
any permanent staff, not to add to their fixed costs. They talk
easily about why they made such a choice: they prefer to keep
overheads down, which makes them freer to concentrate on the

131

quality of work offered. By not hiring staff they avoid dissipating their standard of service.

They talk, too, about how outsiders tend to evaluate 'success'. Does success have to mean big, flashy cars, glamorous homes, and large important job titles? Or can it simply mean a flourishing business, albeit mainly supporting yourself, with a host of satisfied clients?

The last woman featured in this section, even more intriguingly, explains why she is *getting out* of running her own business, returning to work with associates very much as an equal partner. For her, the fundamental problem of paying office rents and the isolation of working on her own, had become too strongly negative. In her mind, there is no sense in which this change of course could be viewed as failure. But again, it leads her to question commonly held views: just what makes a healthy business?

B. J. Harris

ANNE CALLEJA
Link Fortune International:
management training consultancy

IF WORKING FOR yourself is ultimately about gaining more control over your life, perhaps bringing flexibility in exchange for outside job status, then there are those women who seriously question the wisdom of getting themselves enmeshed in paying rent for office space, or in hiring staff who have to be paid every month, whether work comes in or not.

It goes without saying that many women work in a small way as freelancers, or as self-employed, based from home. They are not intending to make very much money, but to keep themselves busy and involved with work which they enjoy – but which leaves them enough time to devote to family concerns as well.

Anne Calleja fits no usual mould. A very hard-driving ambitious woman, she runs an up-market management-training consultancy, based from home. Her income is high, her sights certainly no lower. For Anne, the decision not to pay office rent, nor to take on staff, other than that of working with 'associates' – a network of other freelance trainers and consultants with whom she has been in collaboration for many years – has been carefully thought out. She has a young child, but that has not really directed her choice. More significant to Anne is the priority she places on her *own* skills, the fact that clients are likely to be hiring her work, because they like *her* and want to work with her.

It's an issue that has been raised many times by other consultants. For this woman, it goes towards solving the eternal conundrum about the quality of life.

The long route to going solo

'If I look back, I've always wanted to work for myself. My father was a doctor, and my grandfather was a very good businessman who worked his way up from nothing to owning a shipbuilding company. My great-grandmother was one of the first women in business. So I come from quite an entrepreneurial set-up. My mother always encouraged me to be independent. For her time, she was almost Women's Lib!

'However, for many years, I moved around experimenting with all different types of work. You could look at my cv and say it seems a bit scattered. As I see it, I have carefully pursued a course to bring me to this point in life. My very first venture was to do a Catering Managers' course. I didn't go to university, against my mother's wishes, because I wanted to get out into the working world and thought that catering would be my field. Even back then, I set up my own catering business, cooking dinner parties on a freelance basis.

'Then the opportunity came up to reorganize the catering services for a major company. I'd spent a year in America looking at the fast-food industry. So I decided to go with the times and based it all on the health-food concept, replacing "tea ladies" with bright young students.

'But eventually I decided against staying in catering because the hours are so long. I had discovered I enjoy the personnel side of the work, the hiring and training of staff, so someone recommended that I applied to the Training Board – and that is what put me on this path. I realized then, I could build up sufficient skills so that one day I would be able to work on my own.

'First, I needed more qualifications and so I studied for a DMS, then did a part-time MBA, so that I would have credibility when I set up as a consultant. But, even then, I took a sideways step into education, so I would have a broader base of experience. My father's advice had always been: "Make yourself a marketable product", and this was in the back of my mind. While I was lecturing, and working on my dissertation, I was already doing some consultancy work in graduate recruitment.

'It slowly began to dawn on me that I was already a saleable product. And that's when I decided to set up on my own. I had my Masters degree, good work experience, and I tended to be doing two or three things at once: lecturing, consultancy and the like. I was then thirty-two and widowed. It was time for a change. When I began working it was in Europe and then Malta, where I based myself for a while. My dream of one day having a second home in the sun, so that I could work for six months of the year and then get away for the second half – to write, do research and read – was a fantasy, but I felt I might be bringing it closer.

'One of my clients was a major hotel chain – they invited me back to England to be Management Development Manager for their group here. I was tempted, thinking that I really needed some management and organizational skills. If I wanted to offer that kind of training, I needed to have work experience at senior level. To move on, I needed not just my MBA, but also senior management level experience.'

So how would Anne describe the business she now runs?
'There are many, many women consultants around (and men, of course, in this same field). The women tend to be working at the skills end, offering courses to women returners or on assertiveness training, whereas the men work in organization and development. Well, that is the end where I work. It is a very male-oriented world. Most of my clients are male. But my work is specifically targeted towards helping an organization develop a training programme that is tailored to their business needs. I provide a unique service, because I link the training programmes directly to business results.'

How does Anne, whose business is based in Oxford, bring in the work, from this highly competitive market?

'It is still mainly through recommendation, contacts and networking. I have not yet advertised, nor even put together a brochure, which I'm sure I should do. But recently I sent out a flier, for a new kind of programme I am offering with two other colleagues. It is a totally new concept. I sent out a mail-shot of 4,000. The take-up has primarily come from people who already know me, or who recognize my name. When I rang with follow-up calls, they told me they had responded to my *name*. So it is a personal business, they are buying *you* and your experience, your reputation.'

I was intrigued as to how she managed to keep up such a high-profile status when she works from home. Anne has a young child, and I imagined the usual problems of trying to stifle the baby's cries when she answered the telephone.

'I have never worked from home with the baby there – except in the evenings! I was determined at the beginning to find a nanny, or child-minder, with whom he would spend the day. I was not going to answer the phone with a baby in the background. It's just not on. Anyway, this type of work involves my travelling a great deal. Sometimes I'm away from home for three to five days. I have to work with the client on site. I am very organized. I make sure I have good childcare. My husband is supportive, particularly now he is also self-employed and can be there to help answer the phone. He handles the VAT and accounting for me. You have to plan well.'

How can Anne pursue such a business, on a solitary basis, in the light of all the travelling?

'How I organize that side of the business is the most vital ingredient. I do employ people, but they are all freelancers. My support team is my life. One lady comes in to do all my word-processing. My husband handles the telephone and sales side. The secretary will pick up any incoming calls from the answering machine, and I have a car phone with an answering service. Maybe it still frustrates some clients, if they cannot get hold of me immediately, but I promise to get back to people within twenty-four hours. What's important again is to realize that I am not running a volume business, but a quality personal business. I have developed a very good relationship with my main clients and they introduce me to new work. So far there has not been a problem. Obviously, working in this way means I can keep my costs down, and be very competitive.

'When you're running your own show, the problem is that it is up to you to handle everything: your own marketing, selling, creating new courses, thinking up ideas. But I work with other trainers, consultants who operate as self-employed, to whom I can offer work or they may approach me. It's a question of contracting out to them if the workload is beyond me.

'These freelancers, like me, have a repertoire of skills and I know whom to tap into where necessary. We get on well together. That's how I can remain a one-man band, with minimal overheads, except for the fees I pay them. Although, in my working situations, I have enjoyed managing staff, right now I don't want the hassle of dealing with their problems. I prefer mixing with other freelancers, who know that if the work is not done, they will not get paid. They go to work every day, as I do, prepared to be fired. And we give quality.

'Either I pay them, passing on the fees to the client, or we might go jointly into a big project. The question of how much to charge is always a problem. There was a time I felt I was undercharging and that made me feel resentful, because I realized it came down to my feeling *undervalued*. You have to get the balance right in your mind: is it your work that is being rejected, or the price?'

Anne's earnings are healthy. She explained that her husband, until recently, had gone back to being a student, so she is used to being the major breadwinner. Despite low overheads, her cost of living is high, with full-time childcare to be covered, and her own business expenses. As a service industry, however, one is merely charging for one's time. So how does she cope with the battle to keep fees down, to be more attractive to clients?

'I have a pretty good business plan worked out. I simply analyse what income I need in a month and target work to fit that need. Some of my clients provide long-term regular work. Others may offer a steady contract of one to two days a week. I also work with different trainers on programmes, or earn money through writing, or producing a training video. I do all my costings to clients on a man-day basis, and tell them up front if I am having to bring in someone else, and that their fees will be charged on. On certain occasions, I might be able to use the client's own secretarial services, and telephone while I am on site.

'I was once tempted to grow the business and tried setting up with a colleague. We took office space, but the rent just kept going up and up. I found I had to go in to the office for meetings, and that we had hired a full-time administrator for whom there just was not enough work. Then, when I was travelling, I needed to work late at night on the word-processor, but it was in the office. It just seemed crazy. I was better off based at home. Maybe, if my objective had been to increase the volume of work, it would have worked. But, as I've said before, to bring in more volume would have been to lower the quality of service. But I had to accept I really *like* doing the work myself.

'So many times, I hear clients complaining that they hire a big firm of consultants and eventually find they have been farmed out to a junior. They have felt dissatisfied and I pick up work from their fall-out. They want the person they hired to work on their project. When they know they will have you, and no-one else, you can win big contracts. My clients get value for money, of that I am sure, because my standards are high. And, when they appreciate your work, that's when you get repeat jobs.'

But how does a client know what to expect when they hire an individual consultant?

'Very often, they prefer to see the work in action rather than read a proposal. That is another way I am different. Rather than spend hours of painstaking work putting together long proposals, I prefer to go in for half a day to meet the people involved and to identify their precise needs. They see you in action and can then make a decision. I have heard of people sending out as many as three proposals a week. That is just not cost-effective. My proposals tend to be a letter of confirmation of our agreement!'

How does Anne handle her income, budgeting and find time to develop her own business?

'I work backwards from my overheads: using the amount I need to live on and to invest in my professional work. Each year, for example, I set aside a budget to improve my business practices. This year, I invested in a car phone, a fax and a photocopier. Last year it was the computer. Next year, I'll be upgrading my car. Of course, you go through periods when you worry there won't be any more work coming in. But, to my surprise, this year has been exceptionally lucky.

'On the other hand, that may be due to another investment programme I undertook. Last summer, I took six weeks off work, not to laze in the back garden, though I did a little of that, but to go to seminars, to invest in my own self-development. I plan that, in each year, I will take twenty days of vacation, plus ten days of investment in development and updating my ideas. I aim for a maximum of 120 fee-paying man-days for myself. And I work out from there how much I have to earn.

'In that time last summer, I re-assessed what I wanted to be doing and how to target that type of work. I was very involved in selling, in marketing myself. Maybe that is why I have been so busy. The problem there is that recently, having been so busy, I have not concentrated on the marketing side. You really cannot leave any door unopened.

'Deep down, I love going on courses myself. I adore theory, and will quite happily spend my social time talking shop. I have considered going on to do an occupational psychology degree, or maybe a PhD – but probably not until my forties. There are always new methods to keep up. And on any course there is the networking component, which keeps you in touch with colleagues and with your competition, so there are several different pay-offs.'

Does Anne see herself as a classic entrepreneur? Is delegation a problem?

'Maybe I'm just more of an individualist. I don't see myself as ultra-creative, though I am innovative. But, because of my background in business, I can cover all functions and I understand all general management skills. The important aspect is that even without staff, *per se*, I inspire loyalty. They say that entrepreneurs are bad delegators,

140

are people who want to hang on to their ideas and be in charge. In that sense, I suppose it is true of me.

'But then, too, I'm not in this type of business for money. It is the quality of life that matters to me. I sometimes get very angry when I hear people talking about success. Outsiders see success as a big car or house. But success really comes from within. If you're working for a big company, and you see them creaming off money in foreign bank accounts, and they want you to keep on making a profit for them, you must begin to wonder why you aren't working for yourself.

'I like to have my brain stretched. I need to use both physical and mental energy. It's hard to find the right balance. And although I worry sometimes about money, these days who can say they have security working for another company?'

But does she find in her busy schedule, that she really has more time for her family? Anne laughs, because she admits to being a workaholic.

'Well, I have stopped working at weekends. If I have to be away from home, I try to make that Tuesday to Thursday. Then, I like to leave Monday and Friday open to go to meetings, or for networking sessions in Oxford. I would love to take the occasional Friday off, to go somewhere with the baby and child-minder; or to have my hair done, or do Keep Fit!

'Still, I have my vision that as we have a property on Malta, maybe we'll find a way to live there for part of the year, when I could involve myself in research. In the long run, clients are buying you for your knowledge, so you need to keep up to date; you cannot afford to be worn out, or you'll be of no value. It is interesting that this year has been the most profitable ever, and that was after I took that deliberate time out to work at what I was doing, and where I was going.'

Facts:
Associates: 10.
Full-time Employees: 1.
Freelance support staff: 2 plus husband.
Turnover: Approx. £120,000 p.a.

Daniel T. Pangbourne

YOLANDE BECKLES
3 Circles: training programmes
for women and ethnic minorities

TO BE YOUNG, attractive and black, may not be the only three prerequisites for an easy life. But for someone like Yolande Beckles who, in her late twenties, not only packs a punch in terms of personality, but has also managed to notch several major achievements under her belt, the going has not been too bad. For Yolande, who has been involved with modern dance since she was two years old, maybe the surprise is not only that she did not choose a glamorous type of profession within the entertainment industry, but she has found herself in the world of training.

Although the dance world still potentially holds out new business prospects, to begin with, motivated by a phenomenal early success, Yolande created her own training consultancy, whereby she could focus on the needs of ethnic minorities, particularly of black women, and youth enterprise schemes. Why did someone like Yolande decide to leave well-paying employment and take the risk of going it alone?

'At eighteen, after A levels, not knowing what to do, I found myself working at Sainsbury's. I'd always done a Saturday job there, and though I should have been going on to higher education, I just wanted to leave school. I'd gone for some interviews with banks, but had never been offered a job. So, for a couple of weeks, I went to work at

Sainsbury's on the cash registers. Within those two weeks, I had been promoted to head of store training, and put in charge of training 400 members of staff! It was quite exciting to have such responsibility at eighteen, and the job paid rather well. But after six months, I was bored. I'd been encouraged to go on a management training scheme, where I duly rushed through two years' worth of courses in nine months, and was made a department manager. I was moving round all the big stores in London at that time.

'In 1987, I moved out to Middlesex although I had bought myself a flat south of the river. I wanted to go back into management development, rather than continue in store management. Sainsbury's were very keen on my potential, as their first black woman store manager. But, to make a change, I decided to take up a two-year secondment on a project run by Fullemploy. The aim was to encourage local black people to work at Sainsbury's; not just to take on a "job", but to develop themselves. Black people had such a negative self-image and, because they always ended up just working on the cash registers, it was a two-way road. They were not getting anywhere. Yet I was their token success.

'Already, the doors for black people were beginning to open up. And I was the model black person. My name was becoming quite well known in the industry. As a black woman, I myself had come across a few racial problems in my life, but nothing like the level experienced by these trainees. One of my advantages was that my parents had brought me up to believe in education, to be ambitious, and have self-confidence. I just did not have a stereotyped chip on my shoulder. All I thought was: I had done well and that meant I was good at the job.

'But then I began to question my success. Sainsbury's had deliberately pushed me ahead, whereas other people were still getting nowhere. When I arrived at a new store, people would still ask me if I was the housekeeper, and I'd say: "No, I'm the bloody manager!" So I began to learn, I suppose, more about why other black people had not done well in organizations, and why I, by comparison, had been able to achieve so much. From that learning process, I felt I could pass on my own wisdom. And I began giving sessions on personal development; on why these people lacked confidence and how they could sell themselves to an employer. I began pushing them through towards management levels.

'Five of my trainees became section managers within six months and I was so proud of myself. A lot of them were school drop-outs and yet I spurred them on until they were doing well. By the end of 1988, we won a National Training award. Then I decided it was time to move on from Sainsbury's. I was being head-hunted, and in the end went to work briefly for the Docklands. To leave Sainsbury's after nine years, the new job had to be enticing. Yet, even so, after six months I began to realize there was a niche market out there, into which I could sell.

'Women, and particularly black women, were being ignored. I began to look at training packages aimed at those groups. To begin with, I set up as a freelance trainer. Work began easily, with a six-month contract within Lewisham. I formed the 3 Circles company with my mother, because as the work began to grow I felt that I should be a company, but rather than hire staff I would tap into the services of other freelance trainers. I now work in association with five other freelancers, four of whom are black professionals, who make excellent role models.

'When I walk into a room for a business meeting, because my voice does not come across on the phone as black, I still notice the double-take: 1) because I am black; 2) because I am young and attractive; and 3) because I'm female!

'Now, a year later, the company has already grown to the extent that we are moving into office space. As for secretarial help, I have no-one full-time, but I make use of a secretarial service. Office space has become necessary now, largely to give me premises in which to hold my programmes. I have the money behind me to pay rent. And, in reality, I do now need a full-time secretary and bookkeeper.

'I work alongside the enterprise agencies. I write and sell a lot of unique programmes, many of which are aimed specifically at women starting up their own businesses. I bring in speakers who are also women in business. Black people need a lot of encouragement and help to gain self-esteem. They enjoy being with me because I'm so flamboyant, so totally unshy! The only problem right now is that I'm being pulled in all directions. At some point I will have to stop and look at just where I'm going.'

Yolande the dancer

'Maybe it's because at heart I am a show person, that I make a good trainer. I know how to put on a performance. With a friend and colleague, Sharon Obee, I have set up a dance school across the other side of London, called the Moving Parts Performing Arts School. I had always dreamed of having a performing arts school, for inner-city kids this time, not for the Sloanies. Once you tap into that natural talent, you notice how it helps children find their assertiveness and self-esteem.

'We opened in the autumn of 1990 and all is going very well. We emphasize the child's creative development; not just learning formal technique. The school is open on Saturdays, so it is available to working parents. The children can come for a whole day and do jazz, singing, acting, gymnastics or ballet. Or just for one lesson. It is a private concern, but we aim to be flexible and help out with those who cannot afford the ordinary fees. I know that most mums work, and I just wanted to make sure those kids are not deprived.'

So where does Yolande see herself going?

'I'd hope for 3 Circles to keep on growing. I'll always be around to instigate new ideas. But one day I will step out of the director's role. My future plans include running a nursery for inner-city children, particularly one for ethnic children. I want Moving Parts to become a full-time school, incorporating music.

'So far we have not been involved in any major investment for the school. We rent the space on Saturdays in an arts association building. We hire in teachers by the class. And our families help us run the place!'

Does Yolande see herself as an entrepreneur?
'What am I? I'm a woman who doesn't just talk about what she wants to do, but who does it. Until 1987, I was an employee. Then overnight I became a business woman. I went into that without any market research, with no business plan. I just made it work. My confidence and luck have pushed me through. So far, I feel I am exploiting the two areas in which I know I excel.

'It's important to me that I am seen as a success, especially to other black people. I don't want to be a winner in this year and out by next year. It is crucial for women to know that they can succeed in this type of field, learn how much to charge and how to handle contacts. I set my prices high from the beginning, because I felt I was worth it. Also, as a young business person with no assets behind her, very quickly I learned to ask for a percentage of the fees up front. You just cannot always wait 30–60 days for them to pay. And why should I go into debt because they are slow payers? No, it is the money on the table, or I cannot provide the courses. These are lessons we all should learn.

'Everyone in the recruitment field is wondering where black women are going, and I'm here to help them. Ethnic women no longer have to staff British Rail or the NHS. The world really is out there for our taking!'

Facts:
3 Circles
Staff: 5 and a team of associates.
Turnover: Too early to be exact.
Moving Parts Ltd
Staff: 2 directors and a number of freelance dance teachers.
Turnover: Too early to be exact.

HILARY SEARS
*Sears Langan: executive
search consultants,
now at Boyden International*

MAYBE COMING AS the total reverse of other women whose thoughts
and ideas we have been looking at, Hilary Sears enters the discussion
saying she is not really relevant. After three years of running her
own business, she was, at the time of our interview, changing tack,
moving back into a company – not to be an employee but going in as
an entrepreneurial partner.

Hilary is in her mid-forties, a highly educated and serious-minded
woman, who has already put two prestigious career paths behind
her: the first in advertising before moving into executive search
(head-hunters), following a year she took out in her mid-thirties to
study for an MBA at Cranfield School of Management.

Hilary quickly landed high-paying jobs with leading executive search
companies. But in 1987, she decided it was time to set up her own
small business, pursuing the same business lines. The reasons why
Hilary has now decided to give up running her own business, are not,
in any sense, out of failure, but rather go back a long way: what was
it she really wanted from her work life, and her future?

Her thoughts will be of interest to any woman who has either set up
her own business or is contemplating so doing. Because Hilary's story
raises issues to be considered about the nature of smallness, and of
the implications of 'being out there on your own'.

149

Let us look first at why she decided to go into her own business. She was earning well, not battling for promotion, and there was no young family to consider. Surely she was a woman who had everything going for her?

'The reasons were partly chance and partly circumstance. There was something in me that wanted to give my own business a go; to see if I could really run my own show and be happy doing it. What I have learned is that I have done rather well, but that I just am not happy managing the business aspects any more. I don't want to have to worry about VAT returns, car insurance, BUPA and the Inland Revenue!

'In a sense I have been lucky because, until recently, I had a very supportive assistant who handled all that side of the business for me. In many ways, with her help, I was operating just as I had always done in the corporate environment, without having to face many of the difficulties coped with by other fledgling entrepreneurs.

'There were other major concerns that I never had to confront either, such as raising money. In executive search you have to look at cash flow, but you don't need heavy investment up front. I was fortunate at the outset in being able to take office space, without paying a large deposit, because I rented space in an office being used by former colleagues in advertising. Obviously, I needed certain equipment such as separate phones, answering machine, and my support staff. But everything else was already here.

'I did not put together a business plan to take to the bank manager. Though, with the help of a girlfriend, I did put together a basic business plan, trying to sketch out a cash flow that would demonstrate how I intended to pay my staff if the money was not coming in.

'When I left my previous job, it was taken as rather an emotional decision, and certainly not a deliberate career move. There were no hard feelings, as only seven weeks previously I had been promoted to a partner. At the time, I was also being approached by other firms. I did not take any former clients with me, as that would have been unethical. But again I was lucky as a new client came to me and asked if I would run a major project for them on my own. This meant doing two to three searches for that one client. Aware that I was in a start-up, they agreed to ensure that payment was effected immediately instead of in the usual three stages.'

One of Hilary's biggest concerns in her new decision is the cost of office space, particularly for a low-overhead service industry. So why did she pay rent, could she not have worked from home?

'You could do the job at home, of course. But the bigger firms who are your competition all have very up-market offices, which is important for image. I just knew it would be wrong for my reputation to work from home. I needed a West End address and phone number. But, also, I think I'm the type of person who needs the stimulation of professional peers working around her. That probably is a very big contributor to my deciding now to join another firm.'

But surely she knew that going off on her own carried major risks?

'I had earlier been approached by another firm to come in as their managing director. A colleague advised me then, that if I had the nerve and courage to be MD of that firm, why not run my *own* company? Later, this same colleague backtracked and told me I should not have gone off on my own at this particular stage in my personal life! Her seasoned view was that you needed your personal life sorted out before you set up your own business. It did not in fact worry me, not to have the support of a partner at home, as I have a very strong network of friends and colleagues. Also, by working in the shared office space, with former colleagues, it was almost like being in a company without having them intrude on my business life.'

What were the advantages to going solo? Did Hilary make more money and work fewer hours?

'For three years work has come in, based on my reputation and on referrals. I had been in the world of executive search for five years, and this is very much a business of word of mouth, discretion and trust. Inevitably, as a single operator, you either find a niche area – mine has been in marketing, direct marketing and sales – or you accept that you will operate across the board at a lower level, with salaries that are below the £50,000 benchmark. There are, in that sense, plenty of opportunities for people like myself to go into the middle ground. We have lower overheads and can charge lower fees. But your fee must not be too low, because it would bring into question how good you are. My credibility as a woman in business has never been questioned, more it's whether the client feels they can trust you as a one-person band, and whether you will understand their business.

'The one basic problem of working single-handedly, compared to the bigger firms, is that you don't have the back-up of a team of researchers. That was often questioned when I first met clients. In retaliation, I explained that they would be getting *me* doing the job, not just an unknown researcher, or a junior in the team. I am convinced it is possible to do this work on your own, as long as you have one or two clients using you on a regular basis. One of the biggest problems is in doing one-off assignments, and not getting repeat business; because the workload is so much more extreme.

'In terms of earning, I was always cautious about what I took out, feeling that it was important to build up a reserve against unexpected expenses. I did take holidays because I saw that I owed myself those breaks. But I discovered you are *not* as flexible as you may think you'll be. Running your own business becomes a consuming passion. Whereas your friends imagine you'll have all the freedom and all the money!

'I did think that I would be earning more than when I'd been on a salary. But in the end it was about the same. Initially, when my overheads were very low, then there was more money around. But once you start taking on staff, or premises, then it all gets much tighter. Which is why it is worth looking at the economies of scale. If you are not earning considerably more, and not gaining that much more freedom, then why go through with all the aggravation of the responsibility? Particularly when you consider those areas in which I, for one, was not the least interested: the details of running a business.

'The one plus was that because the corporate pressures were lifted, I found that although I often worked just as long hours, friends noticed that I was more relaxed. Which, in fact, goes against the image of someone running her own business, doesn't it? But then I was not too anxious about money, so long as I did not run into terrible cash-flow problems. I had work, earned money . . . it was the other variables that superseded all.'

The firm Hilary is joining, as a partner, bringing with her a client base and the responsibility of generating her own business, already has prestigious offices. They are the oldest-established search firm in the world, with a team of associates linked up in forty offices across twenty-four different countries internationally.

'I'll be going in very much as a decision-maker, not as a salaried employee without any control. It will be a completely different operational base from being a one-man band. What I realized, as I reached a turning-point in my life if not so much in my career, was that certain basic concerns made me want to rejoin a professional, international team: 1) the economic situation, with the recession making cut-backs in recruitment inevitable; 2) the need to offer clients global coverage. Often independents have link-ups with foreign associates, but this way we have a whole international team and network of offices; 3) the question I had to face was, "what had I really been doing in my own business?" Had I been taking huge risks, had I been genuinely entrepreneurial?

'The answers to those were No. The equation ran, "then why not join in with an already-established firm with partners I respected, liked and trusted".'

Does Hilary not see herself as a true entrepreneur? Does her ego not run to becoming the figurehead of her own company?

'When it is about women running their own businesses, I doubt that ego very often plays a part in the decision. There are so many other contributing factors: such as economic necessity, or because she has taken a career break for family reasons. Many women only realize their potential at the time of a major crisis; then they are forced to cope and to develop skills they did not know they had.'

Had growing her own business been an alternative decision?
'Yes, I would say I was just as strongly on the point of doing that. But I spent a lot of time and thought on the questions involved, talked it over with many friends. I had to accept that I did not relish taking on a hefty loan. To grow a business you have to be prepared to do that. But it seemed like a terrible constraint to me. In expanding I would have to employ others, find another search consultant at my own senior level – and the hunt for that person could take a year or more.

'Either I would have had to go to the bank for a loan, based on my own equity, or I would have had to seek out an investor. If you go along that route, with the equity investor, you may omit the huge personal risk, but you would be talking about a lot of money being tied up in prestigious offices, staffing to the hilt, and all the consequent cash-flow problems. Again the answer to all that was No, in my mind. What I have enjoyed as a single operator is the freedom to run my own business as and how I want.

'But there is another important issue, that I have not as yet mentioned. I am fundamentally a "people person"; I need to feel people around me, even just that someone is there. The interesting exercise for me was to realize: 1) I did not want or need to run the business side of it (none of the VAT details); and 2) that I did not want to work totally alone.

'So when I asked myself, was I prepared to make a longer-term commitment to my business? Was I prepared to upgrade and grow it? The answers again were all No!'

*

What was the motivating force behind the change?

'In the past few months, I have had to move office premises, within the same building, but am no longer sharing as part of the former group. My costs are now much higher, and I lack the compensation of the support team. It really began to seem ridiculous to be paying so much for office space on my own. The assistant, whose fine eye for detail I so much relied upon, has been off on maternity leave. That in itself can be crippling for a very small business. You miss someone you rely on very badly, when it is a temporary break for maternity leave. Not to mention the cost of temporary help.

'Then, too, I had met someone in my private life. Perhaps even more so than before, work did not mean so much to me. Work can become your whole life, if you are not careful. I have known friends set up in business, and the whole working week is absorbed, not to mention weekends too. Work and success in work, of themselves, are not enough to satisfy me. I also need a life outside my office, time to see friends and develop other kinds of relationships.'

Facts (when running own business):
Staff: 2 at the most.
Turnover: Had been running at around £200,000.

Chapter Six

RAISING CAPITAL: SELLING ON

IN THIS DAY and age, maybe it is slightly unwise to talk about a business as flourishing. Nevertheless, there does come a point with any not-so-new company where the owner must consider the choices. What will she do next? How can she either improve the service or quality of product on offer? Or how can she aim to grow the company without going into deep personal debt?

Suzy Frith who set up a PR and Communications consultancy in Northampton; Victoria Barnsley who created her own publishing company, Fourth Estate; Susan Hay, who developed a personal mission into a thriving childcare consultancy and nursery management business; and Prue Leith, who built a small catering business into a huge restaurant and catering services' concern have all gone through such experiences. None decided that she was happiest staying small, or even just sticking with the *status quo*. But each made personal decisions based, in large part, on their private lives and how much time or commitment they felt they could continue to give the business over the next ten years. They also had to decide the level of risk they were prepared to run.

Suzy Frith sought a parent company, a larger London-based concern in her own field, to whom she sold out her equity. She is now in the position of being tied to the parent company for the next three years while she takes her company, FTM Communications, to its expected profit levels. But then for Suzy, in her mid-thirties, the long-term aim is to build in more free time for herself and her plan to start a family.

Victoria Barnsley began her publishing company in 1984 with money raised from a consortium of private investors, when the Business Expansion Scheme was in operation. Undaunted by present circumstances, she is now seeking to raise a considerable further sum to expand her successful company from its current 'small publisher' role to that of a medium-sized quality company.

Susan Hay started out, as have many women, being forced into the freelance/self-employed role when she had very young children, and was unable to afford or find good high-quality childcare. Her expertise in setting up nurseries, her professional experience in town planning and architecture, led to the nascent company being sought out by venture capitalists, to inject money into what they saw as a viable, profitable business.

As Susan herself says, she was forced into 'thinking big'; it was not the first issue on her mind when she initially went off on her own. But these are interesting examples of women who decided not to keep a business small.

Prue Leith, probably the most famous of all the women entrepreneurs in this book, makes a determined call for women to hold on to total control of their businesses. Several very well-known names in recent years have fallen by the wayside, after being seduced into floating their successful new businesses on the stock market. Other names, notably that of Anita Roddick and her Body Shop chain, seem to have mastered the art of continuing growth and keeping the ever-growing mammoth of a business comfortably 'small' in its atmosphere (if not in sales).

But Prue Leith, recently awarded the Veuve Cliquot Business Woman of the Year Award which was previously held by Anita Roddick, seems to hold in her attitude, which is both sane and ambitious, much of the feelings of the majority of women featured in this book. Indeed, as true 'captains of industry', the women in this section, cheerfully still doing well in a difficult business world, are certainly role models to us all.

Paul Lapsley

SUZY FRITH
FTM Communications: public relations and communications consultancy

SUZY FRITH DECIDED to start-up her own PR consultancy, in the field of high-tech business, because she felt dissatisfied with the business practices, hours demanded and ethics involved in the jobs she had taken so far. Married and one day hoping to start a family, she also has to deal with the personal pressures in life made the more complicated by her decision to run what has grown into a sizeable business.

Suzy describes the reasons that led her to seek a parent company; how this type of support and association, with a much larger corporate communications group, would hopefully give her more freedom in her personal life.

Suzy Frith is in her mid-thirties with a business she called FTM Communications based in Northampton. The parent company is the Watts Group in London (formerly known by the name of its owner, Reginald Watts). For someone like Suzy, success in her business life is only one element of the high-priority intangibles: remaining happily married, being in a position to raise a family, and gaining respect through her work are all interconnected.

Why Suzy came to set up her own company is perhaps typical of the experiences of a new, younger generation of business women. She emerged from university, bright and raring to go, only to be gently disillusioned.

'I read History at Kent University, and was unusual in that my husband and I were married at the end of my first year. Neither of us knew where we wanted to live, but after graduating moved to Bristol where I landed a job as a graduate trainee in marketing with a major firm. I found myself in a position with a lot of responsibility. Eventually I was made marketing manager in computer supplies of a smaller offshoot company that they had taken on. The range of activities was very valuable for my experience: I had to source products, put the brochures together, arrange the PR, train the staff, do the lot – and I was only twenty-one! God knows why they gave me so much responsibility, and I did make some hideous mistakes, but it was a great grounding in the profession.

'Then I moved over to the sales side, driving around the country. My husband had moved up to the Midlands, and I was able to base the work from our new home. But, in 1980, I was sucked into joining a few other young people who were forming a micro-computer manufacturing company. I went in with them as their marketing director, with 15 per cent of the shares. Again the job meant driving all over the country. The company should have done well, we had a loan from the Government, and our manufacturing was going well. But, the experience taught me that I would never go into business as a partner again. If ever I went into another business, I knew then that it would have to be by myself. Why? Because we killed each other by *arguing*.

'I found the other people involved to be a very difficult group of men – you do run into some sociopaths in the computer industry! They were a very young company, made up of callow, flash young men, the bright boys newly down from Cambridge. After eighteen months, I was able to get my money out and decided to look for another marketing job. But in the next company I joined, also in computers, I came up against male networking. I wanted to be home with my husband after work, and not go along with them to the pub, which they did not like.

'By then, it was 1984, and I moved to Coventry, to do PR and marketing for a manufacturer of a hand-held computer. During that time, most importantly, my husband decided to give up work, and go back to university, to do a Masters degree in social work, so that he could become a probation officer. At the same time, we agreed that we would try to begin a family. That led to the first of my many miscarriages.

'But then I began to doubt whether it was a good idea to have a baby, at that time, when we had no secure way of supporting ourselves. So, I began to think about setting up my own PR company. Originally, I planned to work as a freelancer, with low overheads, based from home. But very few PR companies around knew much about the computer or the commercial world. As larger clients prefer to be offered an all-round service and press relations was an important side of the work to me, I knew I could not handle all that on my own. I started FTM in 1985, when I was twenty-eight years old. As I was able to take part of my previous job with me, fortunately I had a contract with which to begin. And, more importantly, that meant an income from day one.'

Getting the business started, and watching it grow

'I began very small-time, as a consultant, with hardly any overheads, just a small Amstrad and a second-hand photocopier. I planned to work for a few clients on a retainer basis. But, in fact, the quantity of work overtook me. Within three months, I had employed a secretary and in six months, we had moved into offices. Things just grew. I had to do some cold-calling and direct mail to sell our services, but from there things began to roll. There must be a god who rewards hard work, because business just came in, though not necessarily from those channels I had been pursuing! By 1987, we were attracting bigger clients and we had grown to a staff of four. We moved to offices in central Northampton, and then we began to attract major national clients. By 1988, we had grown to six staff members and are still at that size.

'But by the next year, I began to feel as we completed our third year of trading as a limited company, that although we were way ahead of regional PR companies in terms of volume of business, and trading profitably, any company has to look to the future. You cannot stand still. I had to face the choices of what to do next. The options were:

1) I could go to the bank and borrow money with which to expand, although until then I'd been totally self-financed and had always traded in the black. But I needed to hire some more senior people.

2) I could find a partner, but I knew from my previous experience that could present problems.

3) I could find a parent company, someone who would let me carry on the way we had been doing, and who would offer me a piggy-back credibility. But it also had to be a company that would share our value of being a high-quality service. There are many major PR groups whom I would *not* join. They just chew you up and spit you out. So we had to be careful. I decided, however, on the latter option.'

How does one find a parent company?

'In the first place, I contacted a merchant banker who helped me draw up a prospectus. Finally, after months of agonizing worry, we became part of the Watts Group. Why had I adopted this route? There are several reasons that are a lot more personal than the

161

ones just mentioned. I wanted to build in an exit route for myself, because at some point in the future, before it becomes biologically too late, I do want to try to become pregnant again. My history of pregnancies has been chequered, and I have miscarried more than I like to mention, but I do want to give myself a chance of having a family, try and take sufficient time off so that I can approach getting pregnant correctly the next time.

'Also, I have a fairly short-term view on life. I don't want to see myself running this business as all I do for the rest of my life. I have a yearning to do something different. I love the work, but it does mean I have a lot of responsibilities, both to my clients and to the employees. Someone else has to be groomed to take over. And that is a long, long process. Then, too, after all my hard work, it would be nice to think of recouping something on the effort. Maybe I could take more of a sideways role.

'On a practical level, having the support of the parent group means we can pitch now for bigger contracts. You may need a more well-known company name to bring you that initial reputation, to get you the first interview. One of the major attractions for going in with the Watts Group was that they would push business our way, and vice versa. For them, our positive point is in being a specialist group, working out of London, and therefore we do not charge London rates. With so many corporate headquarters now based out of London, there is potentially a *lot* of work.

'From the Watts Group side, they were looking to grow and wanted to acquire a company in the hi-tech field, somewhere in the regions. They replied positively to the very first circular. First we met in London, and then began on an enormously lengthy process of nego-tiations with the lawyers. Basically, we were the right size for them and affordable. But still it was a fairly traumatic time, trying to keep the work going and sitting in on all those meetings. It gets *very* hairy, as it becomes obvious that your livelihood is also on the line. I was very open with my employees about what was going on. That was the only way I could handle the situation.'

What has been the main effect of being in PR, outside London? Does not having a smart London address instil fear of a lack of sophistication from their potential clients?

'No, not in the kind of work we do, because my staff have so much business experience, with a strong technological base. Sometimes I feel we have been guilty of imagining a problem. Even when I first went to meet the Watts Group staff, I remember thinking to myself, "My God, they're all so incredibly tall!" as though that was a part of their

London mystique. But they too had to learn that we are professionals, not just country hicks. There has been a lot of teasing about where we actually live; and we probably are still getting over the idea of being seen as country bumpkins.

'The parent company have acquired 100 per cent of FTM. I'm on a 50–50 deal with them, so half has been paid up front and the rest we will earn out depending on our performance over the next three years. I am still running the company, very much as my own, but now I am on a salary. Because of the physical distance, and partly because we operate quite differently, I still have more autonomy than many in my position.

'My big hope is that it will make things easier for me in recruiting high-quality staff. Now we can offer the security of a major group. The main problem in being out of London is finding the right calibre of staff.

'On the personal level, the problems certainly have not gone over-night. It now means that I cannot try to get pregnant for three more years. Were I to take time out for maternity, it would mean the business would suffer. And I *have* to bring in a good profit. But apart from that, my staff are probably more secure. It makes our working life more pleasant. And we should be able to attract better clients.'

Recruitment of staff is often a problem for small businesses, but is particularly highlighted when the businesses are situated away from major centres such as London. How has Suzy fared in finding well-qualified, highly motivated people, who also reflect her working temperament?

'I would say that finding good people has been the one major constraint to our growth. I'm looking for such special people, who have commercial experience, sales ability, common sense, and wide cultural reference points. They need to have charm, yet not be wanting enormous amounts of money. But I have discovered that if someone is bright, has spark and commercial know-how, I can train them to write press releases and they learn on the job.

'We are an all-woman team right now. And we get on very well. Sometimes I worry that we have rather a low profile and that being out of London we just cannot network. On the other hand, we work very hard and make good profits. The toughest part is to find someone with genuine PR experience. An agency once sent me a string of men in their thirties and forties, so-called PR experts, but they were really just office drudges. We did take on a man once, but he was too much of a problem; he was rude to people and just didn't fit in. I'm happy with the people I've hired; most of them came by advertising locally. I have tried advertising in the national newspapers, but it has not been very productive.'

163

And what about her role as the entrepreneur, does Suzy carry the major slice of the workload?

'I still do proportionately too much work; a high percentage of the fee-income work with clients comes from me. Clients tend to want to work with me, and it's hard to refuse when you are selling on your name. The entrepreneur does tend to be the one with the innovative ideas and the creativity. Yes, it is an old problem, though I have an excellent number two who is growing daily into the job.

'But my team thoroughly supports me, and I feel I'm a generous employer. Everyone has a car. I try to be flexible with the packages that are suitable to the individual's lifestyle. The work can also be pressured, and at times I know I can be difficult to work with. But we try and keep the atmosphere light and give each other a lot of support. I insist, for example, that we keep our hours normal and I will not let them stay beyond 6-ish. I just won't have us slipping into that awful trap of no-one daring to be the first to leave. We work very hard when we're here, often not taking a lunch break. But there are no rules, my staff manage their own time. I would hazard a guess that most women don't want to work for companies where you are made to attend meetings just as you're about to go home!'

Speaking of her own plans for pregnancy, in an all-woman office, what would Suzy do if her staff became pregnant at the same time?

'You mean if all three who could went off on maternity leave at the same time? I suppose we'd have to close down. I would hope they would discuss their plans with me ahead of time, so we could work things out together. I would like to think we have a flexible enough environment for that.'

Does Suzy feel she is a natural-born business woman, a genuine entrepreneur?

'When I started out, I did all the wrong things. I did not know much about PR, had neither money nor savings, and my husband was a student. We had a mortgage, no assets, but I had learned about running a business from working in two start-up companies. Maybe it is good to throw yourself in like that. Also, at the time, because neither my husband nor I were earning any money, it was quite a relief. There was certainly no competition between us. But I doubt I'd have the nerve to do the same thing now.

'Mostly, I feel it all goes back to common sense. I'm not really the "lass from up North" as they might like to imagine in London. But I do have an instinct about selling, which is what PR is all about. When it comes down to it, if you cannot pick up the phone and get work, you'll be nowhere. You just have to try. No-one likes cold-calling, no-one! I still get the flutters in my stomach, but I have to give it a try.

'Also, I had no idea at the beginning how to cost out jobs. So I took a simplistic approach. We don't bill by the hour, but charge out a daily rate. Our prices are low by London standards. Now that business is tightening up, we can remain competitive. At the moment, we have a very good return on our turnover.

'In PR it is often difficult to say what your turnover is (rather than fee income). But the important point to me is that we make a good profit. It's a question of keeping the right ratio of fee income to overheads. I'm quite lost when I look at a balance sheet. All I ever work on is knowing that I have to earn more than I pay out. Yet I don't think we've ever had an unprofitable month. I do care about the bottom line.

'Of course, we are having to be more aggressive now, as a lot of work is disappearing. But I feel that PR will survive because it is more cost-effective than advertising. I'm determined that we remain useful. I don't think any company should hire a consultant, if the consultant cannot help them make money. We most certainly do not run on traditional gin-and-tonic lines of PR. We help our clients improve their bottom line.'

And what about her feelings about the long-term effect running her own business has had on her personal life?

'I didn't go into this originally to make money, but rather because I wanted control over my own life, and ultimately to give myself more time. However, running a business can be a real burden. So, even now, I find it difficult to go away on holiday; but I'm aware that I should be able to leave my staff to get on with the work. Yet, I think I have gained an inner sense of freedom and flexibility from being in charge.

'The one problem I see in running your own business, is that it can be so *lonely*. My saving graces have been mainly my husband, and, to a lesser extent, the guys who do my graphic design and photography. They run even smaller companies than mine and have been very supportive. I can at least ring them up and ask their advice. From the PR point of view, there may be new jobs on which I feel totally lost. But there is no-one with whom I can share those fears. You can't exactly ring up your head-on competitor and ask for help!

'While I was at university, I lost interest in achieving. But, since going out into the workplace, my natural competitiveness has re-emerged. I tend not to see myself in that way, but I suppose that I must be entrepreneurial. One problem I have had to face is that I am married to a probation officer. That means we have a group of friends, away from my work, and very often I'm introduced with the immortal words: "This is Suzy, she runs her own business," as though somehow that makes me different, or amazing, when really it is quite ordinary to run a business. I suppose I find it quite funny, I mean no-one would ever introduce a man who runs his own business that way.

'Does it mean that I'm different or threatening? Do other women view me strangely? My husband, fortunately, has no problem with my image. And I can always talk over work problems with him.

'But, yes, I do enjoy the good sides. I dress smartly and drive a big car. As soon as we were taken over, I bought myself a sports car, a Mazda MX5. It may feel rather precious, but it's lovely. Right now it fits my lifestyle, myself and the dog – who comes into work with me. I drive a good 30,000 – 40,000 miles a year, and it's important to me that I enjoy the driving. When we have a family, I'll move on to something more sober.

'Time management is an obsession of mine. I'd hate to be so tied up with work that it took me over completely, so I organize my days carefully. I really don't believe work is the most important thing in my life. I try never to take work home or come in at the weekend. Family and friends are very important to me. Quality of life, ethics, these are all priority issues on my list. I wonder if they're as important to a man who runs his own business?'

Facts:
Staff: At present 6.
Turnover: Around £500,000.

Times Newspapers Ltd

VICTORIA BARNSLEY
Fourth Estate:
publishing company

SOME SMALL BUSINESSES are definitely more glamorous than others, especially to the outsider's eye. Whether it is a question of operating a financial services company, marketing maternity and baby clothes, or running your own publishing company, each can have greater or lesser appeal depending on your interests and vantage point. But publishing carries with it a certain in-built cachet.

Victoria Barnsley is already a well-known figure within bookish circles in central London, for having had the enormous gall to take up the idea of running her *own* publishing company, from a starting-point of little experience, when she found herself out of a job because another publisher had gone under. There are other independent *women* publishers. But none is quite as flourishing, nor young, nor has quite the high profile of Victoria. In the publishing industry, women predominate in the number of employees as a whole. There are many more women now at editorial level, even some serving as publisher. But still there are few women on the boards of major publishing conglomerates and even less who are managing directors. Publishing, it has to be said, like newspapers and very often television, gives a greater impression of equality of opportunity than is the reality.

Victoria tells her story: one of a venture entered into almost by accident at the age of thirty. Now, looking back over six years of quite

169

remarkable achievement, she reveals not only how fearlessly she set about raising capital from private investors that first time round; but how she now intends to raise yet more, in a determined launch of Fourth Estate into the stratosphere – from small, to a firmly grounded, medium-sized business.

Beginnings

'I set the company up in 1984, rather by accident, when the publisher I had been working for went bust. I remember thinking: "Oh, God, now I've got to go out and find another job." But, over lunch with a friend, the idea was put to me. It was the year of the Business Expansion Scheme, when private investors could offset their investment against the then-top rate of 70 per cent tax. At the time, I knew that it was a good opportunity, as I would be able to buy some of the contracts from my former employer, where I had been a commissioning editor. The liquidator was about to sell off everything.

'I was also attracted by the idea of being a publisher. It may be cruel to say it, but I think there is really only one interesting job in publishing, and that is being the publisher. The process is all about how to make *and* sell a book. All the different elements come together and have to be made to work. The interesting part comes in overseeing the whole project and making a success out of it. No designer can make a book work on his or her own. No editor, no author . . . no marketing director. They all have to work as a team. The position of publisher means having a finger in each and every pie, including that of the financial organization, and of having basic common sense. I knew it would take me decades not years to make my way up in one of the large publishing houses, so I decided to circumvent the system.

'Yet, I was terribly naïve. I really knew nothing about running a company nor, for that matter, much about publishing. I had not even worked in the industry for long. In a way it was quite cheeky of me to do it; somehow I had the gall. I also did not realize how very difficult it could become. I've been fortunate in that the business has worked out. But then I feel I have had some pretty good doses of luck.

'One thing on my side is that I've always had a good head for figures. They have never worried me. In fact, I rather enjoy looking over the books. I can write, so producing a plan was no problem. I have seen some other business plans, and they are so badly presented that mine would appear to be great literature by comparison. If you can provide a convincing argument for setting up a new publishing house, finding the money shouldn't be a problem.

'Harder is the question of locating good books and good staff. I soon discovered, though, that many people were happy to leave the

170

conglomerates to work for a smaller company. When it comes to salaries, I have to pay decently. There used to be a philosophy in publishing, that you get people cheap because they were so happy to have a job in the industry. But if you pay nothing, a) you won't get the really good people because they will be tempted by the higher salaries in journalism and advertising, and b) you cannot make demands on them when the chips are down. I would say I pay commensurate with the industry, if not better.'

So how did Victoria bring off this great coup?
'I approached various individuals, and said I was planning to start my own company and would they put up some money. Funnily enough, it was terribly easy to raise the money. Because the top rate of tax was 70 per cent, if you invested under the Business Expansion Scheme, you then received 70 per cent of your investment back. Many people were quite prepared to take the risk. When I reached £80,000, I stopped; even to the point of turning down money. I feared that if I raised any more, I would be diluting my own share.

'What I did not realize would be so difficult was how to break into the literary establishment as an "outsider". Being a woman did not help, nor being so young. Becoming established, developing a reputation, they were my major problems. Persuading literary agents to take me seriously was another enormous struggle in the early years. I understand all too well why they were reluctant. As a company we had no track record, and it is the agent's business to represent the interests of the authors, and to get them the best possible deal.

'But I launched by setting up a proper limited company, with directors and a skeleton staff. In the first few years, I took it all very slowly; the main task was getting the name established. I also made design a top priority. I feel that many publishers totally overlook good design, and so we made sure that our jackets and catalogues looked good. That drew attention both to the books and the company. In fact, one of our first catalogues is actually selling in a bookshop in Amsterdam at £5 a copy. Maybe that's the business I should be in!'

But how do you go about creating a reputation?
'The goodwill from the press and media seemed miraculously to be there from the start. We made publicity a strong point and, because we were new, and still had a lot of vitality, we seemed to attract attention.'

*

Did people link her with the feminist press, back in the early Eighties, when they were very much around, simply because it was a woman–run business?

'The truth is that there were so many women's presses around that hardly any women writers approached me at all. They were already being catered for. It was mostly male authors who came to us.

'To begin with we concentrated on political and current affairs titles. The initial idea behind the company had been to fill a gap that existed in the large houses by bringing out current affairs titles very quickly. The small size of our administration meant that we were not hampered by bureaucracy and it was easy to fit books into the list at the last minute. Our first book, for example, was Ken Livingstone's *Beyond Our Ken*, about the GLC débâcle, a book we produced in four weeks.

'So we started off with a political image. But I soon discovered that you cannot run a list based solely on new or hot topics. You don't know when the next one will happen, so that prevented me from planning ahead. Such titles give you a high media profile, but that is not enough to sustain a company. We moved into general non-fiction, and have since branched into fiction. Now we are first and foremost a general publisher.

'To begin with I saw us as filling a particular gap in the market. But the gap I envisage for Fourth Estate now seems to be changing. Most of the larger- and medium-sized companies have been swallowed up by conglomerates. What is needed now are medium-sized *quality* houses, the kind that used to be the mainstay of British publishing. The type of publisher who works well with authors, who operates more like a bespoke tailor than the factory that makes mass-produced garments.'

Are there any advantages in being a small publisher?

'I can tell you the disadvantages first! You don't have such a big cheque book, which means you can lose authors if they demand very large advances. It is always a possibility that even if we have helped make an author's name, that for their next book they will take it to an aggressive agent. The book is then auctioned and there is a good chance that we will be outbid. Which is why I have decided to raise a lot more money, so I have the reserve to dip into should I need to find a huge advance. Publishing has certainly changed since I came in six years ago. I don't know if I'd be so brave today. You need to be much better capitalized. Many are saying that the Nineties will be the decade of the small independent publishers. I hope so.

'In a way, even with the recession, there are still advantages to being small. It is easier to keep control of overheads and the lack of bureaucratic constraints means that decisions can be taken more quickly. Speed of decision making is a great asset in publishing – being first off the mark.'

How did Victoria come about her big breakthrough?

'That came in 1988, when we won the *Sunday Times* Best Small Publisher award. It was a new prize, brought in to launch their Book Section. Suddenly it made us flavour of the month. Every literary agent in town submitted books to us. Unsolicited manuscripts came in by the sackload. It became quite terrible. We worked from a tiny space with a narrow hallway; we just could not get into the building past the bags of mail!

'It is essential to have a break like that. Or a major bestseller. Something that will catapult you on to a different plane.'

But what was it like at the very beginning? How do you sit at a desk with a phone, and become a 'publisher'?

'That first year, it was literally myself and a secretary who came in three afternoons a week, working from one room in a serviced office. Then we slowly built up to a staff of seven, where we are now. At that time, I used a freelance production person, and I did literally everything else. It was good experience. Apart from production, I now know every other aspect of publishing. Few highly paid executives in the conglomerates have that kind of expertise. They tend to move someone over from sales, and expect them to direct the company. But they don't have a clue how the editing process works.

'I began with the contracts I had brought with me, bought in some more, and had to fight to get hold of any decent books. I quite understood that anyone who had written a good book would say to themselves: "Why should I go with an unknown publisher?" But some people were amazingly courageous and very supportive. In our second year, I rang up Auberon Waugh and said to him: "Have you thought of putting your wine columns from the *Spectator* and elsewhere together as a book?" He just said: "Good idea, go ahead and do it." We were able to publish *Waugh on Wine* for a very small advance. He is a big name, and we gave that book all the attention we could muster. In the end he was quite impressed. For us, it was an important book, and we pulled in a lot of support from the media.'

So was progress relatively easy?

'Oh no. There have been times when it has been utter hell and extremely worrying. I have had to use my house to guarantee bank loans. We have gone through some very bad cash-flow problems. Unlike a service business, where really you are just selling your time and yourselves, in publishing you are making huge investments up front

173

all the time. The money invested is big, and the risks are huge. You are gambling on your own taste and interests. It can be very dangerous.

'There have been times when I've woken up at 3 o'clock in the morning, saying to myself: "Oh, my God." I go into a state of panic. It always happens at that time of night, doesn't it? By the time you get up, you've found the courage to carry on again. But I did find the fear very isolating. I've had no partner to support me; I've just been there on my own.'

So, even for someone like Victoria, does running a business take its toll on one's personal life?

'There's a terrible conflict within me for, as much as I need the high profile and enjoy it, there are times when I never seem to be able to escape from Fourth Estate. The problem is worse because publishing is interesting and people want to talk about it. If I was at a dinner party, and I were making washing-machines, probably no-one would want to talk to me. But *everyone* wants to have a book published, or to discuss the Booker Prize! In a way it's fun. Obviously it is interesting to me, too. But it can become quite a commitment.'

She was young and single when she started out at the age of thirty. Did that mean her personal life has been affected?

To this Victoria quickly retorted, 'I'm still young and single!

'That is one of the problems, I never get away from my work. If I were married and had a family, I would find more of a conflict. At the moment, I can handle the full-time commitment, particularly as I'm planning expansion. But, on the other hand, there is no doubt that you are on a conveyor belt when you embark on a business of this nature. You have raised the money, made some substantial investments and you just have to continue. Even if you were to sell out, you would probably have to stay involved for several years as you would be tied in with a service contract. There have been times I have felt almost resentful, that I cannot go off and say "get lost". There is the enormous responsibility to shareholders, to staff and to authors.'

How much time does she see herself putting in to the business?

'Almost all of it. Evenings, weekends, socializing. Dinners and public functions. It is a side of my life I enjoy, but there are problems, like how to take a day off? Ideally, I should be able to take off some time. But I always find that curiosity drives me into the office. I live quite near by, and tend to pop by to see that everything is all right. Consequently, I spend most of my time here. What I need is a hobby!'

*

So why the plans to expand? Many women seem content to keep their business at a conveniently small-but-successful level, without wishing to push the risk factor any more.
But not so Victoria.

'At the moment, I am making the leap from being a fairly small concern, to running a sizeable company with a staff of sixteen to twenty. This means changing everything, including the ways in which I have grown accustomed to managing things. I shall have to learn to delegate more and accept that I cannot become involved in every issue. I want to go from publishing about thirty books a year, to something in the region of seventy. I'm going from small to medium. I shall have to do some major re-organization and hire new staff.

'I have decided to grow the company because when I first started out, it was all a question of having good ideas, creating the product and marketing ourselves well. But, already, I can see that running a successful company of this size is more about managing people, and I want to move on beyond the entrepreneurial stakes. Too often, the great entrepreneurs of our time have shown themselves to be great at starting up, great at the initial idea. But they cannot grow any bigger because they are hopeless at managing people. For me, it will mean being less of a hands-on person and becoming more of a skilful manager.

'Deep down though, I'm still a bit of an entrepreneur. I could imagine selling out of this eventually, and then going off to start something else, something completely different!'

What is it about Victoria that enjoys taking the risks so much?
'I'm a terrible gambler. I play poker socially. I hate to say it, but I do like the buzz of adrenalin. And of course there is an awful gamble in publishing. To counterbalance this, you have to spread yourself broadly, to minimize the risk.

'For example, we might have concentrated more on the export market. A few years ago, the United States appeared to be such a good bet. There it was, five times as big as our market, and many publishers targeted their books over there, while ignoring the home market. But since the dollar collapsed, it has become much harder for us to sell to the States. In the same way, I had to stop being too specialized, or we would have become stuck in one niche. In many ways, though, publishing is about the swings and roundabouts. No-one can foresee what global changes will come about.'

If there was an option to buy her out, would Victoria take that option?
'I'm sure I'd give it a lot of thought. I'd make a lot of money out of it; and until you sell out, there really is not much to be made in

publishing. I don't drive a big fast car! However, I think it would be rather premature to sell Fourth Estate; maybe in five years!'

What about women in business, does Victoria have any thoughts or advice to others following in her steps?

'It occurred to me that people who are *less* confident maybe need more career status as a prop. Men have always needed these props, more so than women. Maybe, therefore, deep down, women are more confident about themselves than men. We just don't need fast cars and status symbols. Maybe this explains why women lack the drive to start their own businesses. Still, there is no doubt that the way girls are brought up prevents too many from becoming entrepreneurs. It's not given any thought. It would never have occurred to me in the past, for example, to set up my own business, though in a way the role of managing director fits me very easily. In fact, I think many more women should start their own businesses. They'd enjoy it, and do well!'

Facts:
Staff: At present 7, but hoping to expand to 16–20.
Turnover: No millions pouring in, she says, but maybe £600,000 this year. By '93, she intends to bring that up to the £3 million mark.

Maggie Murray/Format

SUSAN HAY
Susan Hay Associates:
childcare planning and
nursery management

SOME PEOPLE ADMIT to having 'largeness' thrust upon them. Susan Hay's professional consultancy was still in its slow, growing stage, when she was sought out by venture capitalists – five sets in all – who had foreseen that quality childcare and nursery provision would be a viable business in the near future. Without having to wonder whether she would ever dare go to the bank manager to raise the capital to expand, Susan found herself and the professionally run business in a very different position.

Susan is a serious-minded woman, mother of three children now aged eleven, five and the last just emerging into toddlerhood. But, having built up a professional background in architecture and planning, she herself was at a loss for suitable childcare arrangements. Like many other women, her initial solution was to give up full-time employment and turn to freelance work, at first operating from the kitchen table.

Seeing the need for good daycare for other working mothers, Susan developed what began as a personal interest into a thriving business concern. One clue to her success is that she has come out of a professional background, and her approach has been businesslike from the very beginning. Childcare, as she would be the first to argue, is not 'just' a woman's issue.

*

179

'Originally, I had taken a four-year Business Studies degree, one of the first such sandwich courses that began to open up in the late Sixties. My only motivation was not to become a teacher or a bilingual secretary! But I was always fascinated by the built environment and, on graduating, I joined a planning consultancy in London, using my economic analysis skills, concentrating on the technical side. Eventually I moved closer to the management side, because the practice was flourishing. So, fortunately for me, I was able to develop with them in areas such as project management, programming, and commissioning arrangements.

'But then I had my first child, eleven years ago. I wanted to continue in my job, but there was no nursery around. Already I was convinced this was the way I would wish my child to be looked after, as the ultimate in good-quality childcare. A research group I was in contact with had a workplace nursery, but they had to find it a new home. So I began working with them on finding a new centre. We were looking into Covent Garden, which was being dramatically changed in the late Seventies. I came across a sheltered housing scheme, which had been allocated a social services nursery as part of the scheme. But Camden Council had run out of money for the nursery. We approached them as a private group offering to fit out the nursery and run it for them, in exchange for a peppercorn rent.

'I'm sure they thought we were a cranky group of women. It was quite common at that time to be seen as a "cranky group of women"! All this was becoming increasingly important to me, as I had continued working, but had only been able to tap into informal childcare arrangements for myself. The Chandos Day Nursery in Covent Garden opened with quite a fanfare, and is still flourishing. My son was able to take up a place there.

'Then, career-wise, I moved on to a strategic role with the RIBA, becoming involved with various professional concerns of architects. I had a second child just over five years ago. And, once again, I ran into the same problem. There was no childcare provision available near where I worked. I could not imagine leaving the baby with someone else, and travelling to and from work each day. My job was in central London whereas we lived in Hackney, which adds a lot of time to the working day. It became very obvious to me that I just could not keep up with the job, and raise a family.

'By this point, my older child was in school, so I was also facing after-school problems. There only seemed to be one way to go, and that was to become self-employed, to work freelance from home.'

As she is part of a middle-class professional couple, I had to say that I was surprised she had not taken the full-time nanny option. But Susan has developed strong political feelings about the value of daycare, as opposed to one-to-one nanny or au pair situations.　　　·

'I couldn't really afford a nanny or an au pair, largely because of the expense of accommodation in London. Even with two of us working, we could not have afforded a large enough living space to give room to a nanny; if I had wanted someone living in with us. Also, I did not like the idea of a child-minder. Any social services nurseries were already over-stretched, looking after children at risk or those of single mothers. Both our families live far away from London, so there were no informal networks available either.

'I do feel that to be able to work properly at your job, without worrying about your childcare, is most important. One of the biggest problems to be addressed is that of the middle-class parents who need to work, but who do not come under social services help.

'So I became a freelancer at home, only to learn that even that is quite limiting. It is actually difficult to work with the disturbances of young children, or even to deal with your own attachment. I also grew to feel that one needs a break from work, and should not have work and home life under the same roof.

'But in that time I was based at home, quite quickly I was brought into another project whereby I became Chairman of CityChild, trying to establish some provision in the City for the women working there. CityChild was set up in the Barbican, on an arrangement worked out with Islington Council and developers, London & Metropolitan Estates. First call on places go to stockbrokers' Merrill Lynch employees, but the rest are used by local residents.

'It is very important when embarking on something as complex and multi-disciplinary, as setting up a nursery for working parents, to employ professionals who understand the areas involved. I could see how hopeless it was proving for groups who relied on charities or voluntary organizations. It requires a downright professional approach, the ability to talk the language of developers, builders and planners.

'The success of CityChild led to my being inundated with approaches to become involved in similar projects. I would have liked to have become committed to the cause, but the question was how? If I was to give up my other freelance work, then I would still have to earn a living. So I started charging a fee for the advice that I had been giving on a voluntary basis. And that was how it all began, still based at my kitchen table.'

How did she establish a reputation, or get the 'real' business started?

'It took time before people began to realize there is a professional job to be done in childcare provision. The business community is not equipped to deal with such problems, even if they are interested in creating a workplace nursery. My own interest lies mostly in ensuring that, if we really want *quality* childcare in this country, then we cannot allow the voluntary sector to cope with it all. They can only be one part of the picture. We have to engage private sector money, because the current need for childcare has arisen out of the efforts of the Equal Opportunities campaign. It has grown directly out of the changing role of women in society.

'This is *not* a welfare concern. Nor is it necessarily a government problem. Businesses need women to work for them. Women want to continue their careers when they have children. The two should work together. So, what I was trying to draw to people's attention was the sheer logic of allowing someone such as myself to turn the service into a real profession.

'A lot of our work, for example, is in educating property developers into what childcare can mean for them. We want to enable them to visualize it, and find ways in which it can be sensibly financed to be available to a mixed community of local workers, residents and even on a day-to-day basis to shoppers.'

Hiring your first secretary

'The very first stage of growth is in employing your first helper; that is a more critical step than anything else. At that point, you have someone else's wages to pay. It is no longer just a question of creating enough income for you yourself to get by on. This other person relies on you for her salary. It means you become more organized and have to become more credible as an employer. So, that was when I decided I needed an office, to get away from the shop, to try and spend more quality time with the children and not always to have my mind elsewhere.

'My secretary and I rented space in Omnibus [Gillian Harwood's Workspace development], which was perfect for starting up, as it meant I did not need to invest in photocopiers and the like. For a year, we worked as consultants on a retainer basis for Midland Bank, helping them with quality standards on the 300 nurseries they were setting up. In fact, it was landing that contract that gave me the confidence to take the space at Omnibus and make the move away from home. The combination of suddenly having a sizeable contract and an employee gave me the boost.

'Our main reputation has always been as consultants and it will remain that way. But then we began to be approached by the first in a long line of venture capitalists. They were keen to make use of my experience and reputation to set up a string of nurseries. At the time, I had a viably healthy consultancy going, and I was not looking to expand. One day, I did have in mind building a flagship nursery of my own making and creation, but I had gone no further than imagining asking the bank manager if I could borrow a little!

'That is why I say that largeness was thrust upon me. I was encouraged by outside investors to "Think Big". In March 1990, just a year after we moved into Omnibus, we received substantial financial backing to develop a nursery management business alongside the thriving consultancy.

'The latest group of venture capitalists were agreeable, because they recognized the importance of the consultancy continuing to have a life of its own, so that it could provide the necessary introduction to nursery management. There is still a great deal of education to be done on the impact of childcare on the business sector.'

Why does Susan feel so strongly that the business community needs educating about childcare provision?

'Because they have to understand before going ahead *why* they are having a nursery. If not, a few years hence, they'll be asking the question and then deciding it would be better to have a gym instead. The furniture will be ripped out to make a gym (for all the workers!). That is why they have to understand the implications of childcare, that it is not just bottom line, but that its virtues may be measured in terms of "softer" benefits. Only out of that way of thinking will we get good long-term childcare.

'This is a version of social cost-benefit analysis. We are talking about permanent childcare as an investment in future generations. For all the well-rounded reasons. We don't want only the private sector to look at the current demographic crisis, or skills' shortage, because that is also short-term. Much more is involved, such as how they can become good employers and what their female employees' lives are like outside the workplace. They are not just putting Elastoplast on a brief economic sore!'

How did the capital raised change the business?

'We have been able to expand the staff dramatically. We have an education director, a financial controller and manager of administration. I now handle overall strategy, manage the business and direct the network of expert consultants. We're becoming more multi-disciplinary every day. Our aim now is to tap into the best experts in each field.

'Hiring staff of quality and calibre is very costly. I have an assistant who takes on part of my consultancy work, which was important, because a few months after the business grew, I took time off to have my third child.

'Since that time, we have already built and opened (in September 1990) our first flagship nursery in Floral Place, next door to the new offices where we are now located in North London. The nursery places are filling up nicely and we're delighted with the way it has turned out. Now, we can operate a nursery on our own terms. We can change the educational programme as we learn new things, and put different ideas into practice without having to go elsewhere for a budget. It also means, when negotiating with clients, that when we receive them here, we can show them exactly what we are talking about. Also, being in the heart of Islington, we are busy building strong ties with the community.'

But, being quite a costly concern to parents, I suggested that the nursery was not exactly there to serve the community.

'It is private, and independently run. One local employer has taken on a few places. It serves many local people who work in the West End and the City. We are running a training programme with local child-minders, and we liaise with schools so that we can find out all there is to know about the transition from nursery to primary school. We also communicate with all the local voluntary organizations. It's very much a two-way concern. One thing that has delighted me is to have offered nursery places to the local Education Authority, who are having such a hard time recruiting teachers.

'The nursery is open from 8 a.m. to 6.30 p.m., available to children from six months to five years. It is all-day care, with a strong educational emphasis. The cost is £130 a week, which is competitive in central London. A nanny can cost people up to £200 a week gross, plus live-in costs.'

But how do they foresee making great profits? Childcare would seem at the outside to be rather a non-profitable business.

'The profits, in terms of the venture capitalists, will only begin to come in when we have created a lot of nurseries. You cannot hope to make a profit out of just one. But we elected to go with this group of investors, because they were not just looking for a fast payback. They understand the need to work from strong foundations. The set-up costs of a nursery are substantial. The increasing salaries for staff who are a scarce resource are in themselves major investments. Right now, the burdens we are carrying are great. We are running three management contracts for other nurseries and, within twelve months, we will have

184

four more nurseries up and running. Our business plan suggested that within a few years our goal should be forty nurseries. The nurseries are named after their local community so, for example, this one is Floral Place: a Susan Hay Associates nursery.

'New business comes in by our approaching property developers, showing them how we could take some space and develop it into a nursery. At first, there has to be an element of financial risk, to enable us to grow.'

But is venture capital a less risky way to go, for Susan herself, than taking the loan out from a bank?

'Not really. We're playing with bigger stakes. At first, it can sound like a fairy godmother has come to find you. But, of course, it is not like that. There are a lot of strings attached to the money; 1) it means giving up part of the ownership of what you have created, and 2) it brings you into a new league with a board, who probably have a less idealistic view than you. I'm now a director of a company in which I have part-ownership, but no longer total ownership. In return, for equity, you give up rights and control.

'But the capital brought with it an opportunity, without which I would not have been able to invest in major projects. Otherwise, I would have had to personally risk my home to raise the money. Venture capital gets you out of the personal assurances' risk, which can be a major problem for anyone wanting to expand.

'Yet still there are difficulties. One day you are on your own, and the next, suddenly you are beholden to people who have a totally different financial interest. That requires you to go through a speedy learning process. However, the rigour it brings to the business has to be good. You become more commercial and go over all decisions twice. You can no longer be led quite so much by your heart.

'The other side is that it reflects well on your business ability, that you were able to negotiate the venture capital in the first place. It was a lengthy and expensive project, which was undertaken during my pregnancy. One thing that should be pointed out is that if, in the end, we had not gone ahead with the capital – considering the amount of time it took and the expense of solicitors and accountants – it could possibly have killed off the business. I'll never quite know if that forecast is true. But no-one should go into it lightly.

'Although we have our competitors in the market, indeed now there are many, we are an attractive proposition because we are so professional, and we know how to deal with the "big guns" out there.'

*

185

As we finished talking, the recent quote of Margaret Thatcher's about her vision of workplace nurseries leading to a nation of children, 'being dragged across cities to their nurseries' was brought up. What did Susan think of such a pessimistic outlook?

'I now have a workplace nursery. My baby has a place next door. He's a year old and he loves it. He's never happier than when going in there. A great deal of research has been done that shows that provided the *quality* of care is right, day care can be very beneficial to the child. That is the key issue: quality. The nurseries have to be set up properly, by professionals, not done on the cheap. They are not a dumping ground for parents who don't want to be bothered with their children. They are not simply a convenience for mothers who would rather be at work than "at home". They are a positive benefit to the child, that we should not overlook, and a positive benefit to society. They are helping to raise our future generations.'

Facts:
Staff: 16.
Turnover: £350,000.

PRUE LEITH
Leith's Restaurant
and Leith's School of Food and Wine

THERE ARE MANY success stories in this country of businesses run by women whose names are not on our lips every day, yet if we hear their name mentioned, we might say, 'I'm sure I've heard of her, or maybe I saw something recently about her on television'. I would hazard that Prue Leith is one of those people.

Prue Leith runs a highly respected business, made up of her restaurants, cooking school, catering business, cookery books, journalism and her role as adviser on foods. She has deliberately not over-extended or over-expanded her company, but maintains a determined control over its every aspect. After all, she says, the businesses all carry her name; and that should continue to mean something.

Briefly, the South African-born Prue Leith, now just turned fifty, has taken a tiny one-woman catering business, run from a bed-sitter in Earls Court, into a £7 million a year turnover group: Leith's Restaurant, Leith's School of Food and Wine, and Leith's Good Food (catering that includes venues such as the Queen Elizabeth II Conference Centre, Kensington Gardens Orangery Tea Room, Hampton Court Palace and most recently Leith's in Hyde Park).

In the Caterer and Hotelkeeper's list of the top 100 companies, her catering arm ranked third among competitors in pre-tax profits and fifth in sales per employee. The group also owns much of the freehold

189

property from which they operate, making a substantial contribution to their tangible assets which stand at well over £3 million. Leith's Farm Ltd, in the Cotswolds, was bought as a country base for recipe development, vegetable production and for promotions. The companies are all owned by Prudence Leith Ltd, run by Prue herself as managing director and her husband Rayne Kruger.

Prue Leith's busy portfolio also covers broadcasting, lecturing, writing, and serving on the boards of major companies. For five years, she was a part-time member of the British Railways Board, specially concerned with revamping their catering services, and she also serves on the board of Argyll, the parent company of the Safeway supermarket chain. Currently, she is one of the twelve-member team on the National Training Task Force of the Department of Employment, and on the Duke of Edinburgh's Commonwealth Study Conference for 1992. In 1989, she was awarded the OBE for services to good food.

In conversation, Prue Leith is charming and very understated. You feel a strong sense of purpose and some of the determination that must have been there to make this apparently accidental success story quite so remarkable. But maybe one of the secrets to her success lies in a keen interest in hard work, and less of a fascination with the fruits of success or her own ego?

'I'm often asked for my views on why certain women do so well in the world, and the one tip I can give is to say, "Don't get married. Or if you are going to marry, leave it until later by which time you will already have a career under your belt." These things are obviously easier said than done, but there is something in the thought, particularly if you are eager to build up a career. You just may not find the time to marry at that stage of your life if you are very busy or motivated. It's far wiser to focus your energies on career than to be out hunting!

'For myself, I did not marry until I was thirty-four. There is no doubt in my mind that having a husband and then children slow you down. Of course, since I was then in my mid-thirties, I found it very nice to be slowed down and to realize that scrambled eggs in front of the television are a real luxury. But I doubt I would have achieved so much had all that happened to me in my twenties. When Rayne, my husband and I were first living together, I had to calm down on some of my efforts.

'For example, I used to make pâté for pubs which meant setting the alarm in the middle of the night to turn the pâté over. That sort of long slow cooking always happened at night, and he refused to tolerate the smell of pigs' livers for my terrine cooking away in his sleep any more! Not only did he not approve of the alarm clock going off in the night, and my padding downstairs, but to this day he will not eat terrine or pâté because of the smell!

190

'The other side to the equation was that being a South African, and living in London, I was quite a misfit. I just was not part of the middle-class tradition that meant I would go off to the countryside at weekends. Consequently, I found myself pretty much alone, and would happily work on Saturdays and Sundays.

'But the other reason, I suppose, has to be called *ambition*. Women tend to avoid the word, although it is quite all right for men to be aggressive and ambitious. Women tend to hide that streak in themselves. In my case, ambition is just the desire to do the next thing. I cannot resist jumping in and making something work. A friend of mine is mad keen on Wagner operas, but I knew nothing about Wagner. So off we went to the Bayreuth Festival. I just find the idea of doing anything wholeheartedly a terrific temptation.

'That same characteristic, I will confess, has also brought me into deep trouble. Like my present concern with the catering in Hyde Park. I said to myself when the contract came up, "I could run the Park catering better than anyone else." It seemed important to me that decent food should be available in the London parks. But I have learned that it is genuinely an enormous problem. We now have the three-year contract which includes running the Dell; we have also invested an enormous amount of money in refurbishing the New Serpentine restaurant, and there are the mobile kiosks.'

How did Prue begin the business?

'At twenty-two, I launched myself as a caterer, making dinners for housewives at £3 a time, from my Earl's Court bedsit. Fortunately my landlady had no sense of smell, so she did not realize I was cooking. Many people go into business with a friend, and then it all falls apart when the friendship breaks up. But I worked on my own, and when I reached the point of being able to employ people, I paid someone else to do the driving. I have never had a partner. If you get used to running a business by yourself, to making your own decisions, it must be very hard to change.'

But the big question was why Prue Leith has steadfastly fought off going public?

'I just don't want shareholders making decisions for me. My husband is my financial director and, in many ways, he has proved a great restraint on some of my wilder ideas. We operate cautiously. When we married, he was a novelist and historian. He is many years my elder and it was he who taught me my first lessons in accounts, how to keep a cash book, just the simple basics. To this day, our accounting system is based on a simple double-entry bookkeeping system. I have never understood anything more complicated, and we are finally computerizing the whole system which is spread out around the different arms of the group. Each division has always been run separately, and only now are we going to integrate it all. But I do like to keep my eye on everything.

'One of the reasons for our financial success must be in Rayne's knowledge of property. He encouraged me to put all our profits into buying the freeholds of our business properties, so now we are a much more solidly based company with no sizeable borrowings. When you compare us with those companies who have been caught in a trap of buying and borrowing recently, they have fallen because they just cannot keep up with the interest rates.

'We have only ever borrowed on a small scale. When I had run my catering company on a very small scale for five years, for example, I had saved enough money to contemplate opening a restaurant, which meant I only had to borrow £12,000, and with a little family money I was able to launch. Then, when we opened the Cookery School, that cost £750,000 to set up, and we did incur some borrowing. But it was done on the strength of the freeholds that we already owned. The school is already paid off. The basis of our company has always been very sound. I would say I have a very childish Mrs Thatcher-type of fear of borrowing. It's the housewifely thing of not spending more than you have in the purse.'

So how did the company grow to be so big?

'I would say first that we are not really very big. Just because the company is run by a woman, it leads people to wonder and marvel. But, in the same time that I have been in business, someone like Sir Terence Conran has made and lost several fortunes far larger than mine. We only turnover £7 or £8 million altogether, and I have been in business for twenty-eight years. We have just steadily and slowly expanded. If I were a man it would not be seen as anything remarkable, and you certainly would not be interviewing someone like me!

'I did not come into this with any great plan. We have none of the structures of larger companies, no targets or five-year plans and financial budgets. The general idea is that you make as much money as you can and give good service. You try to control the costs, that's the only message I give my managers. I never say to myself, "In five years' time, the retail division will have eighteen contracts," or such like. I'm sure I probably should, but I just tend to respond to challenges that are put in front of me; more so than sit down and think to myself, "I must go out and get a contract for such and such." Usually, in fact, I am asked to put in a tender for any new contracts available.

'Having said all that, when I do undertake a new project I approach it with great energy and care. I do not like things to go wrong,

192

because my name is up there for all to see. I am certainly egotistical and *hate* complaints!'

But why hasn't she become like Laura Ashley and opened a Leith's on every High Street?

'People occasionally put that idea to me; I think it is a question of wanting to stay in control. Because I am egotistical, I don't want anything to move out of my control. For that same reason, I won't take on contracts out of London, except for near Oxford where we have the farm. I will not take on anything that I cannot physically go and see. I know I wouldn't have the time to be running all over the country. The furthest away I deal is at Hampton Court. I make a determined effort to go there once every couple of weeks. I book myself to go around all our units in the City. I make sure I visit and know just what is going on in all our "empire". By comparison, if you asked Rocco Forte, he probably would not know if he even owned certain hotels, let alone visit them all.'

So that brought us back to the question of why they have deliberately avoided going public. Did she, like many women, prefer to keep her company reasonably 'small'?   Husband- Strong influence

'Yes, and my husband also is not keen on expansion. Because he is older, he feels we should have our priorities based on ensuring our lifestyle is comfortable and that we have a good time. I used to travel all over the world just because I was invited. I do find it hard to say, No. But now, as I grow older, I do appreciate staying at home myself and going out to the farm at weekends to ride my horse.

'Obviously the natural way of a business is to grow and by now we would be on the USM (Unlisted Securities Market), because we are not a very big company, but we have a very good name. But the downside of that would mean my having to attend all those tedious meetings, which takes up a lot of time and does absolutely nothing for catering. At heart, I am a cook. Most of my time, I worry about the quality of our food or service. I do not spend time worrying about where the money goes overnight.

'But I am very determined not to go public, unless perhaps I wanted to retire or get out of the business altogether. Then, maybe, I would grit my teeth and bear it for the three years while being floated or being bought out by some major company. But, even then, I'd be most concerned because the name is our biggest commodity. I would not want to drive past some restaurant with my name on its doors, and see it was either stone empty, or not living up to our standards.'

193

Despite her protestations of smallness, the various arms of the group are so wide and encompassing, add to that her family and outside concerns, just what sort of day does Prue Leith work?

'I do a lot of running around to all the businesses. Let me see, a typical example from my diary in June: I took my daughter to school on Monday morning, and did a television appearance. Then I went down to Hampton Court for the opening. I threw a birthday party for my husband's ex-wife at the New Serpentine Restaurant, which we had just opened. That evening, there was a business dinner at my restaurant. The next morning, a breakfast consultative board meeting for Air Europe, then a TEC meeting; then I spoke at a conference about training in the afternoon. That evening, it was dinner with Sue Lawley and Lord Armstrong at the restaurant, which was purely social. Then, I went to the memorial service for cookery writer Jane Grigson. I had to give away school prizes, and then look in at the Catering Company building. Then I lectured at the Cookery School, and finally attended a meeting with Safeway store managers.

'Generally, I'd say I spend about one day a month at the Cookery School. I still love teaching, real hands-on teaching with the class. It gives the students a chance to meet me, and I do remember when I was at the Cordon Bleu School feeling that we seldom saw Rosemary Hume in the flesh.

'But, at the moment, most of my time is being taken up by the Park catering. The whole business of staffing, of what to do when it rains, or when it is too crowded and busy on sunny Sundays; and how we cope with the litter and the graffiti; these considerations are all totally time-consuming. Do you know that in Hyde Park there is chewing gum under every single table, every day. But in Kensington Gardens there is never any gum under the tables!

'The saddest thing is to realize one doesn't visit the places that are running well. I have hardly been round any of my City units for several weeks, because they are just doing so well, and I am confident in their work. I had to write a company newsletter on that theme recently, in case they felt I was ignoring them.'

So what about the question of her family and how she has blended her many roles as wife, mother, and business woman? Prue has a fifteen-year-old son, Daniel, now away at Eton, and an adopted daughter from Cambodia of the same age, called Li-Da.

'I must tell you, I am most proud of something my son said the other day. Because he is at Eton, he is only home occasionally. But before that he was a weekly boarder. Once both children were out at school most of the day, I found I could devote more energy to my work. One day, Daniel read an article about me as a great business woman. He said, "Mum, you're not really a business woman, because you're always at home." And I thought, "Ha, fooled you." They see me as someone who is always at home, in my jeans, cooking in the kitchen. The fact that my children don't really believe that I am a business woman means I'm not forcing it down their throats. They don't see me rushing off at 7.30 a.m., briefcase in hand.

'But if you look at the way my business has grown, it follows the pattern of my domestic life. It grew rapidly until I had children: the catering company, the restaurants and then the school were all opened. Then Daniel was born and we adopted Li-Da. For ten years nothing much happened outside. But as soon as they were at boarding school, the retail division began to expand, and the contract catering arm doubled in size.'

What would she suggest as the secret to her success?
'It's energy, I'd say. You have to be boringly energetic. I'm the kind of person who has to have projects. I'm sure I must be tiring to live with sometimes. Even when I was recovering from an operation, and imagined I'd take six weeks off doing nothing, I managed to complete an enormous patchwork quilt. I never take time to read during the day, not even the newspapers, because it feels so much like wasting my time.

'I do a lot, but I hope not to the extent that I'm frazzled, or that I have no time for my staff and their children. Some people are so busy being the executive woman that it all becomes a joke. Both my husband and I work from the office in Kensington, which is in the same building as the restaurant. We have a flat near by, and the farm in the country.

'Apart from the personal side, I'd say we succeed because we are service-oriented. There is a style to our food, and we indoctrinate all our staff in Leith's own style (which is very simple and does not mean cutting radishes into roses!). The business grew out of my love of cooking. But then I discovered I love the business side, too. My father was a corporate man and my mother is an actress. I rather assumed I'd follow in her arts side, but find I really enjoy business.

'I like winning. There is a great joy in making money. Many cooks will say they are not in it for the money but, if you can't make money from the trade, then you'd lose all the pleasure. Because, like it or not, money is society's stamp of approval. I get a real buzz to see the weekly report and know where we are making a good profit.

'I believe in quality food and, quite boringly and passionately, believe that whether it's a sandwich, a hot dog, or a three-course meal, you should prepare the food with good ingredients and that it should be fresh and delicious. Even a sandwich should have the best available bread, best butter, best cheese, etc.'

Facts:
Staff: Full-time, nearly 350.
Turnover: From a turnover of £709 in her first year, Leith's group has an annual turnover of £7–8 million.

EPILOGUE

WITHIN A WEEK, as I was finishing up this book, two very different meetings with women occurred. Much of my time these days is spent in various networking capacities, meeting interesting women who are either involved in the business world at large or who run their own businesses. The first such chance meeting showed that, beneath her bright smile, the woman's tale revealed the type of enormous problem that might beset enterprising men and women today.

Over lunch, among a group of women she had never previously met, this brave soul let it be known that she and her husband were about to lose their home. They had been in the restaurant business for nearly thirty years. They had overborrowed against their home, and now the building societies were refusing to ignore the growing default in interest payments. 'We have nothing,' she tried to say cheerfully.

But, I wanted to know, how had they managed to borrow so much, so unwisely, against a home they had in fact owned for the same thirty years; against a mortgage that if only left untouched would by now appear ridiculously low? Refusing to criticize her husband, perhaps for foolhardy actions, she resolutely defended their decisions as being 'jointly made'. She had not been coerced into rubber-stamping the agreement.

But I came away from that lunch feeling quite disturbed. There was this woman in her mid-forties, with two grown-up daughters now leaving home. If the business had been hers, if the financial decisions had rested in her lap, I asked myself, would she have put her (their) home at such risk? Most women are far more sensible than that. The home is one area we know to be sacrosanct. Business achievement, success, status, probably rank far lower than domestic or even emotional happiness. My gut feeling was that if only they could go back over the years, turn the tables so she was the financial partner in the business, they might yet have been doing very well. There is an inbuilt sensibleness about women, shown in the pages of this book, that may prevent them from reaching some of the external heights – in terms of business success – but at the same time will cushion them from some of the lows.

The second woman was also in her mid-forties, with a different kind of story, though none the less human. Now a successful solicitor, she had only turned to this profession when she dropped out of her first career path, on having her children at around thirty. Once qualified as a solicitor, she set up what became a successful business. Three years ago she decided to join a well-established firm.

Expecting to hear that the reason for such a move was because her own business had hit hard times, I was surprised at her answer to my question, 'why?' 'Because I wanted to make more money,' she said with refreshing honesty. Running her own business had proved immensely satisfying, but ultimately exhausting. The problems to some degree had outweighed the advantages, which were of course flexibility and the chance to build up a business along the lines she desired. So when her high-profile business was sought by a larger company, she decided the time was right to be bought out.

But, she made an interesting point: to her mind, the positive advantage of having run her own business for a few years was that she had been able to move up several notches in the career stakes; bring herself to a level where other companies had taken note of her expertise, where she had become a much more marketable commodity.

Running your own business can, therefore, be seen not so much as a final move, the ultimate expression of one's worth and capabilities, or even limit your future prospects. For a woman, particularly, who may have family issues to juggle, taking the entrepreneurial gamble can be seen as a reasonably short-lived venture that enables her to 'grow' her own status, put herself on the map, flex her muscles and show the outside world that – even without the normal c.v. or track record – she is enterprising and certainly someone to be taken seriously. And running her own business may mean she is much more in control of her life.

The women who feature in this book are all leading examples of the courage, determination, initiative, drive and resilience necessary to take an idea from its inception, nurture it through the growing years, help it grow into maturity until, finally, the new business has become part of the community. Enterprising Women are only now coming into their own. We'll certainly be seeing a lot more of them in the future.

Appendix:

COMPANY NAMES
AND ADDRESSES

[in alphabetical order]

BLOOMING MARVELLOUS: *maternity and baby clothes by mail order*
VIVIENNE PRINGLE AND JUDY LEVER.
7, Galena Rd,
London W6 0LT
(081–748–0025)

BRIDGEWATER: *pottery and ceramics*
EMMA BRIDGEWATER.
739, Fulham Rd,
London SW6 5UL
(071–371–9033)

THE BUSINESS RESEARCH UNIT: *corporate and market planning*
ANNE RIGG.
5, St John's Lane,
London EC1M 4BH
(071–251–5566)

DOW-STOKER:*management and women returner training*
LINDA STOKER.
The Mill,
Stortford Rd,
Hatfield Heath,
Bishops Stortford, Herts CM22 7DL
(0279–730056)

JUDY FARQUHARSON LTD: *recruitment*
JUDY FARQUHARSON.
47, New Bond St,
London W1
(071–493–8824)

FASTRACK: *computer supplies*
NUALA FORSEY.
5, Avro Court,
Ermine Business Park,
Ermine St,
Huntingdon, Cambs PE18 6YA
(0480–433839)

FOURTH ESTATE: *publishing*
VICTORIA BARNSLEY.
289, Westbourne Grove,
London W11
(071–727–8993)

FTM COMMUNICATIONS: *PR consultancy*
SUZY FRITH.
79, Overstone Rd,
Northampton NN1 3JP
(0604–232223)

GRAMMA'S: *Original Herbal Pepper Sauces*
DOUNNE ALEXANDER-MOORE.
Unit 6,
Acorn Centre,
Hainault Industrial Estate,
Hainault, Essex IG6 3TU
(081–501–3530)

GROSVENOR INTERNATIONAL: *commercial/residential real estate*
JAN MORGAN.
The Gate House,
6, Erskine Rd,
London NW3 3AJ
(071–586–0088)

SUSAN HAY ASSOCIATES: *childcare planning and nursery management*
SUSAN HAY.
Floral Place,
Northampton Grove,
London N1 2PL
(071–354–9945)

LEITH'S: *restaurants and catering services*
PRUE LEITH.
94, Kensington Park Rd,
London W11 2PN
(071–221–5282)

LINK FORTUNE INTERNATIONAL: *management training consultancy*
ANNE CALLEJA.
12, Bushy Close,
Botley,
Oxford OX2 9SH
(0865–864679)

PHIPPS PUBLIC RELATIONS LTD
PENNY PHIPPS.
Woburn Buildings,
1–7, Woburn Walk,
London WC1H 0JJ
(071–388–2525)

FIONA PRICE AND PARTNERS: *financial advisers to business and professional women*
FIONA PRICE.
33, Gt Queen St,
London WC2B 5AA
(071–430–0366)

SEARS LANGAN: *executive search consultants*
HILARY SEARS.
now at:
Boyden International,
24, Queen Anne's Gate,
London SW1H 9AA
(071–222–9033)

TAYLOR: BENNETT LTD: *specialist placement consultancy for advertising and PR*
AIRDRE TAYLOR AND ANNITA BENNETT.
Dorville House,
John Princes St,
London W1M 9HB
(071–408–2449)

3 CIRCLES: *training programmes for women and ethnic minorities*
YOLANDE BECKLES.
Unit 40,
Cannon Wharf Business Centre,
35, Evelyn St,
London SE8 5BJ
(071–231–9901)

UNITED WORKSPACE: *managed business centres*
GILLIAN HARWOOD.
United House,
North Rd,
London N7 9DP
(071–700–0288)